The Habana C̶ ̶kbook

one for Hearts of Palm
Red onion
avocado
tomato
Olive oil +

Florida A&M University, Tallahassee
Florida Atlantic University, Boca Raton
Florida Gulf Coast University, Ft. Myers
Florida International University, Miami
Florida State University, Tallahassee
University of Central Florida, Orlando
University of Florida, Gainesville
University of North Florida, Jacksonville
University of South Florida, Tampa
University of West Florida, Pensacola

The Habana Café Cookbook

Josefa Gonzalez-Hastings

Edited by Andria Kuzeff

4·04·05

Enjoy!
Jo Hgstg

UNIVERSITY PRESS OF FLORIDA
Gainesville/Tallahassee/Tampa/Boca Raton
Pensacola/Orlando/Miami/Jacksonville/Ft. Myers

09 08 07 06 05 04   6 5 4 3 2 1

Library of Congress Cataloging-in-Publication Data
Gonzalez-Hastings, Josefa.
The Habana Café cookbook / Josefa Gonzalez-Hastings ;
edited by Andria Kuzeff.
p. cm.
ISBN 0-8130-2737-3 (p. : alk. paper)
1. Cookery, Cuban. 2. Habana Café. I. Kuzeff, Andria. II. Title.
TX716.C8G66 2004
641.597291—dc22   2004045150

The University Press of Florida is the scholarly publishing
agency for the State University System of Florida,
comprising Florida A&M University, Florida Atlantic
University, Florida Gulf Coast University, Florida
International University, Florida State University,
University of Central Florida, University of Florida,
University of North Florida, University of South Florida,
and University of West Florida.

University Press of Florida
15 Northwest 15th Street
Gainesville, FL 32611-2079
http://www.upf.com

This book is dedicated to my family.
To the loving memory of my father,
Emilio, who always encouraged me to do what
I wanted and believed that I could.
To my mom, Flor, for teaching me
appreciation and love for all things beautiful.
To our dear family friend Maritza Smith who,
when I need help, steps right in and has never
made me feel like a burden. And finally,
to my husband, David, for going along with
the restaurant idea, against his better
judgment, and for being there every
step of the way.

"Cuba—this is the most beautiful land
that human eyes have ever seen."

Christopher Columbus, October 28, 1492

✒ CONTENTS ✑

ENSALADAS SALADS

PLATOS PRINCIPALES MAIN DISHES

VEGETALES VEGETABLES & ACCOMPANIMENTS

POSTRES DESSERTS

BEBIDAS BEVERAGES

༼ FOREWORD ༽

With this recipe book Jo Gonzalez-Hastings extends an invitation to readers to try her native food. In doing so she hopes her readers will see Cuba as it once was, an island of gaiety, friendship, and fine dining. Jo's recipes are the favorite dishes of the Gonzalez family, collected over the years, as well as Jo's innovative additions to the family's Habana Café menu.

The Habana Café in Gulfport, Florida, draws diners from nearby St. Petersburg, the Gulf beaches, Sarasota, Orlando, Miami's South Beach, and northern Pinellas County. The cozy dining room is artfully decorated with colorful scenes. Jo and husband David, a CPA with an office next door, can be seen during restaurant hours working tirelessly at the front counter, sending menu requests on to the kitchen.

Diners at the café find themselves returning often for golden brown plantains, a selection of shrimp dishes, flavorful chicken, unusual rice as a side dish, warm Cuban bread, and picadillo, a Cuban favorite.

Jo spends some time each day at their lovely home in Pasadena, frequently cooking for coffees, teas, and dinners for local fund-raising organizations. She is a generous contributor to the Florida Orchestra, Museum of Fine Arts, Infinity Club for Abused Children and Adults, Science Center, and Boley Centers for Behavioral Health. Another group, a favorite charity, is Save Our Strays, because Jo is an animal lover. She has three pets with "special needs." One is a large Flemish rabbit with bad rotator cuffs who walks around like an otter. She also has a blind cat, and another who is a diabetic.

Flor Gonzalez and her late husband, Emilio, brought daughter Jo out of Cuba in 1965, first staying in Mexico for nine months, and then making their way to St. Petersburg, their ultimate destination. The family fondly remembers the pre-Castro days in Cuba and a special restaurant, La Zaragozanna, which specialized in seafood. They credit it as the source of true Cuban food.

"But much has changed with the food since those days," Jo says.

On my first and only trip to Cuba in 1980, I found dinner entrées were usually eggs, and when requesting coffee after a sparse dinner at a café on the Malecon walkway along the bay, I was told by the maitre d', "We have no coffee but we are trying to get some."

Jo Hastings is definitely able to translate her innovative cooking talents into a book for discriminating readers who are ready to learn about interesting cuisines. You will find true Cuban food in Jo's recipe collection, and you will find that Cuban food is as satisfying as any.

Ruth L. Gray
Food Editor and Restaurant Critic, Retired
St. Petersburg Times

✍ ACKNOWLEDGMENTS ✍

This book is the direct result of so many people in my life, past and present. Many are the thanks that are due.

To Kate McKean, who took the time to listen to me about my ideas for this project and, with great insight, led me to Andria Kuzeff, who really made all of this happen. Her guidance, patience, and belief in me and this book are heartfelt. How can I ever thank you enough?

In the early inception there was just me, and then along came this great photographer, Jennifer Holcombe, whose relentless efforts and terrific energy survived a year and a half of party after party and food shot after food shot. Jen, thanks for sticking it out with me.

To the University Press of Florida and Meredith Morris-Babb, one can only dream of opportunities like this. I am not only thankful, but so very grateful. To me, this is a moment of greatness, and how can anyone thank you for that?

To Tom French, it's not every day a novice writer like myself receives encouragement from a Pulitzer Prize winner. Thank you for your kindness.

To my staff at Habana Café–there is not enough time in a day to thank them. Their loyalty is overwhelming. My staff loves our food and they are our best salespeople. We came a long way together, and I am very fortunate to have them. My kitchen manager, Horace, has my deepest gratitude for all his daily efforts to ensure our continued success.

To my loving family, who have kept me connected to my roots through the stories and the cooking. When we left Cuba in 1965, I left with a child's heart, and my parents left with such hardship, but somehow, we made it. I love all the memorable stories of my mom and her sisters. They tell of the magic of Cuba, how it once was. When they talk of the nightclubs and the restaurants, you can see my mom's eyes light up. "Fantasy" and "marvel" are her two favorite words to describe the island left behind. To my mom and all her sisters, thank you for sharing the stories and for teaching me by example how much fun cooking really is. It is my favorite hobby.

Thanks to my cousins Amy and Josie Rodriguez for doing some research for me. It was a great help. To my aunt Alina, who is such a passionate cook, thanks for sharing a few of your specialties with me. To my great-aunt Titi, her memory lives with me in the writing of this book. I clearly remember the soups she used to make. They were so comforting.

To my cousin Manny Rodriguez, thanks for all you do for my mom, "La Mima," and me. To my wonderful aunt Edelmira Gonzalez, what would we do without you?

To my friends who have helped me along the way to insure the success of the restaurant by keeping me "grounded." Ruth Lyons and Marissa Zoda, a thank-you is not sufficient. Your friendships mean the world to me.

There are not enough words to thank Maritza Smith, who for the past twenty-five years has always been there for me. To her devoted husband, Harley: Pops, I love you. Carlos Aguila, your friendship is a bright light.

To Pat Saunders and Captain Ed and Maggie Gonzalez, my food purveyors, thanks for putting up with my demanding ways. Your patience ensures Habana Café's success.

To my loyal customers such as Mr. and Mrs. Potter, Danny Carlin and his daughter Kathy, and her husband Ray, seeing you all in there week after week, year after year, gives me great pleasure. For that, I thank you.

To Mark Larsen and the lovely Mrs. Larsen, you have made such a difference in our lives. I feel lucky to have friends like you. Dwayne Allen Vallario and Zoe Ann Dufour-Hofmann, our journey from childhood to adulthood has been a blessing for me. To Oilda Ortega, your love for Cuban food is truly an inspiration.

And finally, to my husband, David, who encouraged me to write this book. Thanks for making me believe it was possible to be published. You have all my love.

The Habana Café Cookbook

My father's mother, Olivia, in 1935.

✍ INTRODUCTION ✍

In my Cuban family two things were always certain—food and good times. I am fortunate to come from a long line of cooks. My mom, who is the foundation for this book, and all of my aunts taught me that cooking is a fun and gratifying experience. I surely learned by example and took the two things I love, food and entertaining, and turned them into a successful business. I opened the Habana Café in Gulfport, Florida, to celebrate my heritage with authentic Cuban cuisine and my memories of the good times with family, friends, and cooking, and I believe *The Habana Café Cookbook* will do the same.

When it came time to select the pictures for this book, the food pictures were easy. I thought the family ones would be too. My mom and I started looking through all of the pictures of old Cuba and pictures of her heyday, and it was sad for both of us. For her, it was all those memories of a life that once was and for me, a life missed. She lived through the grandeur of what Cuba had to offer at that time. As we were looking through mountains of pictures, I mentioned that we missed an opportunity to visit Cuba when the pope was there a few years ago. With teary eyes, she said, "*Lo que ojos no ven, corazon no ciente* [What the eyes can't see, the heart doesn't feel]."

The loss she feels, even to this day, is devastating. I asked her if she would, under any circumstances, ever go back, and she replied with a staunch, "Never."

Having lived through the Bay of Pigs and the Cuban Missile Crisis, she and my dad said good-bye to Cuba through the window of an airplane bound for Mexico. Their Cuba no longer exists. Castro has turned what was once a tropical playground into, at best, a third world country, where the people live in homes with dirt floors and have little food or clothing. That realization is very painful for both of us, and closer to the Cuba that I remember.

After the 1962 embargo, food was hard to come by, and for years, we routinely ate only poached eggs, rice, and beets. I had a pet duck as a child that my

My grandfather, my mom, and her sisters. From right to left, Tia Niña, Tia Chirin, my grandfather Luis Escalona, my mom, Tia Bunny, and Tia Nene.

Aunt Alina at her fifteenth birthday party in Cuba. Cuban girls celebrate their fifteenth birthday, as American girls celebrate their "Sweet Sixteen."

mother told me flew away. When I was in my thirties, she told me our family had to eat it. Every three or four months, we were rationed one steak per family member, and one pound of sugar every six months. My father went hungry so his wife and daughter could eat. When we arrived in the United States after nine months in Mexico awaiting our visas, my five-foot-ten-inch father weighed ninety-six pounds and had exactly twenty dollars in his pocket to begin our lives in America. We stayed with family in Miami until my parents were able to find work and begin looking for a place to call home. They fell in love with the small town of St. Petersburg, or as my dad liked to call it, "San Petesburgo," which became our home.

Food is still hard to come by in Cuba. One customer, returning from a visit to Cuba, wanted to know why we did not serve a particular dish he had enjoyed there. I went upstairs to speak with him, and he was just gushing with his stories of Cuba. "Oh, you have to go, it's unbelievable, the people, the sights, the food."

I asked him what he ate and he told me that he dined at the home of some people who had turned their home into a makeshift restaurant. He said it was real home cooking, but only for tourists with U.S. dollars. He had eaten white rice, fried green plantains, and *jutía*.

I looked at him and asked, "*Jutía?*"

"What kind of Cuban are you that you don't know what that is?" he asked.

I told him I was really embarrassed and would ask my mom. I ran downstairs and called my mom at home.

"Mima, *jutía*." She heard that and she said, "Oh no, you have them at the restaurant, call an exterminator right away."

I said, "Mima, you're not listening to me, I said *jutía*."

"Yes, yes, I heard you. Get rid of them before you have a rodent problem," she said.

I was getting frustrated, so I took a breath and said, "Mom, listen to me, there is a gentleman upstairs who just came from Cuba and said he ate *jutía*. How come I've never heard anyone in our family talk about that dish?" I asked her. There was a dead silence on the other end. "Mom?"

"Oh, *dios mio*," she said, "those are fruit rats, big fruit rats." In shock, she said, "Just tell him you couldn't get ahold of me, don't tell him what he ate."

My mom on her favorite horse, Don Quijote. This was taken at the family ranch, Bayamo, in December 1945.

My mother at the family house in Santa Fe, September 1949.

My first Christmas, eleven months after Castro took power.

Mima, Pipo, and me at my first birthday party in January 1960.

This photograph of me was taken in Mexico City in September 1966, shortly after we left Cuba. Every time I make *ropa vieja* [old clothes] I remember this little dress, because when we left Cuba, we were only allowed to take the clothes on our backs and one change of clothing. Needless to say, when we got to Miami after nine months of wearing the same thing, the clothes were in shreds.

My fourth birthday with my aunt Edelmira, "Tia Niña."

I hung up in disbelief. I went back upstairs, and yes, I lied, and told him my mom was not at home.

"Well," he said, "maybe next time I'm in town you'll be able to tell me." I excused myself and went back downstairs. To this day, I just cannot believe it, but as for my mom, she believes it.

As for me, I hope to see a Cuba *libre*, a free Cuba, so that I may someday return and see my birthplace and maybe, in my lifetime, the grandeur that my mother remembers. This book is my effort to capture how my family feels about the country we left behind and to share with others the beauty of authentic Cuban cuisine. Habana Café was simply a dream a few years ago, and now it is an established restaurant that brings me great pride. My restaurant, where there is hot sauce on every table, blends exotic food and local art for a warm family atmosphere for our customers to enjoy. It is a restaurant built on customer loyalty and employee dedication. Nothing is more gratifying than a happy customer, and I offer this book to all those customers who have asked me for my recipes over the years. *The Habana Café Cookbook* contains both the recipes used in the restaurant and some family favorites passed down to me over the years.

About Cuban Cooking

Cuban cooking combines elements from several cultures—the Spanish, the Africans, the Chinese, and the Indians. Traditional Cuban foods have been flavored by the ancestry of the land. With each new group of immigrants to the island came their knowledge of foods and their preparations. Cuban food is a culinary blend of European and other cuisines, from the Spanish conquistadores, the African slaves, the Asian laborers, and the Indian natives of the island. To limit Cuban food to yuca, picadillo, and black beans and rice is to miss out on much of the history of Cuba and its people.

Cuban food on the island is very different today. Since the revolution, Cuba has been more concerned with feeding the people than with fine dining. In 1990, when Castro declared "The Special Period," Cuban cuisine received another blow by being cut off from the communist world that had subsidized it. The island nation found itself struggling to survive on its own.

In the last few years, pressured by thousands of tourists and a government that wants U.S. currency, food production is increasing. But even the hotels cannot guarantee a consistent-quality food product. Their main seasoning is salt, because all other seasonings are scarce.

Although Cuban food is not as popular as other cuisines, such as French or Italian, some Cuban specialties like *lechón asado* [roast pork] would certainly be savored by gourmets around the globe. People are beginning to notice Cuban food more and more. It has been brought into the spotlight by such celebrities as Gloria Estefan and Jennifer Lopez, who have opened successful Cuban restaurants.

Nuevo Latino cuisine in the United States is growing up, right along with the exile communities. More and more chefs are introducing the former beauty of Cuban cuisine around the country with restaurants like Victor's Café in New York and Alma de Cuba in Philadelphia. American entrepreneurs, such as Steven Starr, see the allure of Cuban cuisine and the potential of taking traditional foods and putting a spin on the recipes, with things such as corn nuts, sage, shittake mushrooms, and goat cheese. This concept of fusion cooking mixes native ingredients with new ingredients not common to the traditional recipes. I use this technique to modify some family recipes to be more appealing to my American customers. The traditional accompaniments to Cuban dishes are black beans and white rice, ripe or green plantains, but there are certain traditional foods that you have to have an acquired taste for, such as yuca and malanga. With the exception of Fondas in Miami, most Cuban restaurants have modified their menus to accommodate the American palate. I have two menus, my Cuban menu and my Nuevo Latino menu. It is the best of both worlds, and my mother would not have allowed me to shortchange traditional Cuban food. Like she says, "Cuban food done right rivals any other cuisine in the world."

In the glossary at the back of the book, I provide detailed information about the common ingredients I use to prepare the dishes that have made Habana Café a success.

✌️ SALADITOS ↝

APPETIZERS

Cocktail parties have become a very popular form of entertaining. They require a lot less preparation and are less expensive than a dinner party. They can be as small or as large, as simple or as elaborate, as you wish.

The following recipes are a part of my catering business. They are easy to put together, beautiful to look at, and very satisfying. Some will be perfect for a cocktail party, while others are more suitable for a sit-down dinner.

ENDIVE WITH HERBED GOAT CHEESE

If you are short on time, local gourmet stores have wonderful selections of cheese spreads. Almost all herbal cheeses will taste great on endive.

8-ounce package goat cheese
1 garlic clove, minced
2 teaspoons fresh chives, chopped
¼ teaspoon salt

¼ teaspoon white pepper
4 heads endive
Chives or watercress for garnish

Beat first 5 ingredients at medium speed with an electric mixer until well blended. Trim the bottoms of the endive so the leaves are about 3-inches long. Use approximately ½ to ¾ teaspoon of the mixture on the bottom of each leaf. Goat cheese is rather soft so you can spread the cheese easily. Garnish with chives or watercress, arrange on a serving platter, and refrigerate until ready to serve. *10 servings/40 pieces*

WATERCRESS MINI-SANDWICHES

5 thin slices white or whole wheat bread   *1 bunch watercress, washed and snipped*
3 ounces soft cream cheese   *Grape tomatoes, optional*

Remove crusts from bread. In a food processor, mix equal amounts of cream cheese and watercress. Spread mixture on bread. You can garnish each mini-sandwich with either a sprig of watercress or very thin slices of grape tomatoes. It is easier to cut sandwiches in half after you have put on the spread.

5 servings/10 pieces

CUBAN SANDWICH

I think the greatest mystery of Cuban cuisine is the Cuban sandwich. There are so many different variations of it that everybody is confused about what a traditional Cuban is. If you ask people in Tampa, a Cuban is not a Cuban unless it has salami, lettuce, tomato, and mayonnaise. If you ask my mom and Maritza, they swear that it is just mustard, the pickles, Swiss cheese, and the sweet ham and pork. "Salami," they say, "that's an Italian hoagie."

I clearly remember the first day we opened the restaurant, and this gentleman came in and ordered ten Cubans to go. He was taking them back to a construction site. While he was waiting for the Cubans, he asked me who did my sign for the building. I answered him, and said that I thought they had done a great job. He said, "Yeah, the letters are real nice, but they misspelled Havana. They put a *b* and not a *v*."

I explained that the correct spelling of the capital of Cuba is indeed with a *b*, but he wasn't buying it.

"This is the first time I've ever seen that," he said. So if that was not enough for him, here come the Cubans off the press, with no salami, lettuce, or tomato. I could not believe the look on his face.

He said, "Wait, there's no salami, lettuce, or tomato on there."

"No," I responded, "these are traditional Cubans. The salami, lettuce, and tomatoes are Tampa-style." He walked off with a puzzled look on his face. When he got outside the restaurant, he looked up at the sign and shook his head again, still in disbelief.

My mom and Maritza say that the recipe provided here is the authentic Cuban sandwich, and I am sticking with them.

1 loaf Cuban bread	9 ounces sweet ham, approximately
2 tablespoons mustard	6 slices
Dill pickles, thinly sliced	9 ounces roast pork, thinly sliced
3 slices Swiss cheese	1 tablespoon melted butter

Trim the ends off the loaf of bread and cut it into 9-inch sections. Cut bread in half lengthwise. On bottom half of the bread, spread the mustard, and put 4 or 5 pickle slices on top of the mustard. Then layer cheese, slices of ham, and slices of pork on top of the ham. Place the other half of bread on top and cut in half at an angle.

Preheat oven to 350°F. Place sandwiches on a nonstick baking sheet and brush the tops of the sandwiches with butter. The traditional Cuban sandwich is always pressed. You can achieve the same effect by placing a heavy cast-iron skillet over the sandwiches, or by using a waffle iron. Bake until cheese melts, approximately 6 to 7 minutes. Cut into quarters.   *4 servings/4 pieces*

ELENA RUZ

This sandwich was named after a patron of a once popular restaurant in Habana called El Carmelo, located in the area of Vedado at Twenty-third and G Streets. People went to this gourmet café for *cafés* [coffees] and *bocaditos* [sandwiches]. Elena Ruz was likely an American whose last name was Rush, which Cubans would have pronounced as Ruz. She was a frequent customer of El Carmelo between the years 1945 and 1948. She always requested this *bocadito*, an unusual combination of cream cheese, turkey, and strawberry preserves, which was not on the menu. The staff began calling the sandwich the Elena Ruz.

You can also toast the bread if you like.

2 slices white bread, crust removed	1 tablespoon strawberry preserves
1 tablespoon cream cheese	4 ounces cooked turkey

On 1 slice of bread, spread the cream cheese, and on the other slice, spread the preserves. Add the turkey and close to make a sandwich.   *1 serving*

FINGER SANDWICHES

1 loaf white or whole wheat bread, crust removed
Cheese slices or basil leaves for garnish

Egg filling:
1 cup hard-boiled eggs, finely chopped
2 tablespoons onion, finely chopped
¼ teaspoon salt
⅛ teaspoon white pepper
2 tablespoons mayonnaise

Ham filling:
1 cup sweet ham, minced in a food
  processor
2 teaspoons pimentos, finely chopped
2 tablespoons mayonnaise

Spread each filling on 4 slices of bread. Add either cheese or basil leaves for garnish. Place another slice of bread on top of each and cut in half.

8 servings/16 pieces

ANCHOVY AND CHEESE MINI-CIRCLES

10 pumpernickel bread slices
2 teaspoons horseradish
5-ounce jar Old English cheese spread

5 anchovy fillets, cut into strips
5 pimento-stuffed olives, sliced

Using a 2-inch round cookie cutter, cut circles from each slice of bread.

In a bowl, mix horseradish and cheese spread. Spread mixture on each circle. Top with anchovy strips and olive slices.   *5 servings/5 pieces*

SALMON ON MINI-BAGEL CRISPS

3 ounces softened cream cheese
20 mini-bagel crisps or thin slices white
  bread, crusts removed

3 ounces sliced smoked salmon
Fresh dill

Spread cream cheese on mini-bagel crisps. Cut salmon into slices to fit the bagel crisps. Garnish with fresh dill.   *10 servings/20 pieces*

SHORT-ORDER APPETIZER

Grape tomatoes
Fresh basil leaves
Fresh mozzarella cheese, cubed

Olive oil
Salt and pepper to taste
Cocktail picks

Drizzle tomatoes, basil, and cheese with olive oil and salt and pepper to taste. Place one tomato, one basil leaf, and one cheese cube on a cocktail pick.

Each pick equals 1 serving

CUBAN BAGUETTE

½ loaf Cuban bread, in ¼-inch slices
Olive oil
3 cups bleu cheese

1½ red onions, thinly sliced
Dried basil

Brush each bread slice with olive oil and sprinkle with bleu cheese. Broil until cheese begins to melt. Top with slivers of red onion and dried basil sprinkles.

10 servings/20 pieces

MUSHROOMS AL AJILLO

2½ pounds button mushrooms
5 ounces olive oil or butter
　(10 tablespoons)
3 garlic cloves, minced

Salt and pepper to taste
3 tablespoons chopped parsley
¼ cup chablis

Wash mushrooms and dry well.

Heat olive oil or butter in a frying pan, sauté garlic for 1 minute, and then add mushrooms. Add salt, pepper, and parsley. Cook for approximately 5 minutes, then add white wine. Stir occasionally.

Cover and cook another 5 minutes, until mushrooms are tender. Serve.

6 to 8 servings

STUFFED MUSHROOMS

30 medium mushrooms
½ pound pork sausage or chorizo, with casing removed

¼ cup Italian bread crumbs
½ cup mozzarella cheese, shredded

Wash mushrooms and remove stems. Chop stems.

In a skillet, over medium heat, brown sausage or chorizo. Remove and drain.

In same skillet, still over medium heat, cook chopped stems until tender, about 10 minutes. Remove skillet from heat, and stir in sausage or chorizo, bread crumbs, and cheese. Stir until everything is well mixed.

Preheat oven to 450°F. Fill the mushroom caps with the mixture. Place on a nonstick baking sheet and bake for 15 minutes. Remove mushroom caps from baking sheet and put on a serving platter. *10 servings/30 pieces*

AVOCADO APPETIZER

3 avocados
2 tablespoons butter
2 tablespoons water
2 tablespoons sugar

3 tablespoons white vinegar
2 tablespoons Worcestershire sauce
5 bacon slices, cooked and finely chopped

Cut avocados lengthwise around the seed, and gently twist to separate halves. To remove the seed, strike it with the blade of a sharp knife so the blade lodges into the seed, and twist to lift out the seed. Peel and slice avocados.

In a medium saucepan, bring butter, water, sugar, vinegar, and Worcestershire sauce to a boil. Reduce heat, and simmer for 15 minutes, stirring occasionally.

Arrange avocado slices on individual salad plates. Spoon hot sauce over the avocado and sprinkle with the bacon bits. *6 servings*

SCALLOPS WRAPPED IN BACON

2 pounds sea scallops (approximately 28)	14 bacon slices
	Toothpicks
¼ cup chablis	Lemon for garnish
1 tablespoon Badia complete seasoning	Parsley for garnish

In a large bowl, mix scallops with the white wine, and sprinkle with complete seasoning. Gently mix until all scallops are coated. Set aside in refrigerator until you are ready to wrap them in bacon.

Preheat broiler. Cut all bacon slices in half. Take each half and wrap around a scallop, securing it with a toothpick. On rack in broiling pan, place the scallops side by side. Broil 3 inches from top, for 8 to 10 minutes, turning once. Place scallops on serving platter and garnish with lemon and parsley.

NOTE: You may substitute shrimp for the scallops, and they will take less time to broil. *8 servings*

FRITURAS DE BACALAO (CODFISH FRITTERS)

1 pound codfish	2 tablespoons parsley, minced
4 eggs	¼ teaspoon freshly ground black pepper
6 tablespoons flour	1 lemon, sliced into wedges
1 teaspoon baking powder	2 cups vegetable oil, for frying
3 tablespoons onion, minced	

Fresh codfish is preferred. If you are using salted cod, soak fish overnight. Lightly boil in fresh water the next day. Drain fish and remove any bones and skin.

Beat eggs. Crumble fish and combine with eggs and remaining ingredients, except lemon wedges and oil.

Fry tablespoonfuls of this mixture in hot oil (375°F.) until golden brown. Drain and serve with lemon wedges. *8 servings/24 pieces*

These are probably my favorite appetizers. No one makes them better than my mom. Every time we had guests over, she made these croquettes. They are great finger foods and delicious. She did not make them very often because they were time intensive, but when she did, my dad and I were right there waiting. We would scarf them down like there was no tomorrow. I would call my childhood friend Dwayne and tell him, "Hey, Mima's made croquettes," and he would drop the phone and come over. He would walk through the front door with this gleam in his eyes.

"Where are they?" he'd ask.

"Oh, Pipo and I ate them already," I said. To this day, Dwayne swears that in the thirty years we have known each other, he has eaten exactly two croquettes.

"Amazing," he says.

I think he is lucky to have gotten that many.

4 tablespoons butter	*½ teaspoon black pepper*
1 cup all-purpose flour	*2 cups Vigo Italian bread crumbs*
2 cups milk	*3 eggs*
3 cups minced ham	*7½ cups vegetable oil for frying*
¼ teaspoon Badia complete seasoning	

In a large saucepan, melt the butter over medium heat until butter looks foamy. Add flour and blend. Gradually add milk until mixture is well blended and thickens into a paste. Add the minced ham, complete seasoning, and black pepper. Cook for 2 minutes, stirring constantly. Remove from heat and cool at room temperature.

On a work surface, spread a layer of bread crumbs. Take some of the ham mixture, about 1 tablespoon, and roll it in your hands to make a sausage shape about 1½-inches long and about ¾ inch in diameter.

In a medium bowl, whisk 3 eggs. Take each croquette and dip it in the egg wash, then roll in bread crumbs until covered.

In a large skillet, heat vegetable oil to 375°F. Put the croquettes in the skillet and cook until golden brown. Remove from skillet to a dish lined with paper towels to drain. You can hold the croquettes in the oven at 200°F until ready to serve.

NOTE: You can also substitute chicken for the ham. If you do, just add 1 tablespoon chopped parsley to your mixture. *10 servings/30 pieces*

Here are some of my favorite dips for vegetable trays:

BLEU CHEESE DIP

⅔ cup milk
1 cup sour cream
½ teaspoon Worcestershire sauce

1 dash hot pepper sauce, or to taste
4 ounces bleu cheese

In medium bowl, mix all ingredients, cover and refrigerate until ready to serve.
Yield 1½ cups

YOGURT AND CHEESE DIP

8 ounces cream cheese
½ cup plain yogurt

½ teaspoon salt
½ teaspoon dill, fresh or dried

In a small bowl, with a mixer, beat cream cheese until smooth. Add yogurt, salt, and dill while mixing. Blend thoroughly. Put mixture into serving bowl and serve. *Yield 1½ cups*

SOPAS
SOUPS

My dad loved soups and my mom loved making them. When we first arrived in the United States, my parents had very little money. They pinched pennies to save enough money to buy a house, so that meant a lot of soups. Soups are very economical and very satisfying. Our favorite was Ajiaco, a Cuban Creole soup made with beef and our favorite roots. A bowl of Ajiaco and toasted Cuban bread, drizzled with olive oil and sprinkled with salt, made a very hearty meal.

After some time in the United States, my mom learned to make soups other than the typical Cuban soups. She became rather sophisticated in the soup department. She loved experimenting, and we loved trying everything. On cold winter nights we ate these great soups like garbanzo and navy bean, and of course lots of black beans and rice, and on hot summer nights, we ate wonderful cold soups that were refreshing and interesting. I hope you enjoy the following soup recipes as much as my family and friends have.

FRIJOLES NEGROS (BLACK BEAN SOUP)

The following recipe is a combination of my mom's recipe and a few nontraditional additions of mine.

1 pound dried black beans
4 bay leaves
1 green bell pepper

1 red bell pepper
2 small onions

To begin, you will need 1 pound of dried black beans, rinsed and picked over.

If you choose to soak your beans overnight, do so by covering them with cold water and add 2 bay leaves, ½ green pepper, ½ red pepper, and 1 small onion, halved. Remove any beans that float to the top. Be sure to remove the bay leaves, peppers, and onion before boiling the beans.

The Goya brand of dried black beans are of very good quality and it is not necessary to soak them overnight.

In a large soup pot, add beans and enough water to cover beans by about 3 inches and bring to a boil. Add 2 bay leaves, ½ green pepper, ½ red pepper, and a small onion cut in half.

For the *sofrito:*

⅔ cup olive oil	1 teaspoon cumin
3 garlic cloves, minced	2 tablespoons onion powder
½ large onion, blended	2 tablespoons Badia complete seasoning
½ green bell pepper, blended	¼ cup tomato puree
½ red bell pepper, blended	¼ cup chablis
1 teaspoon dried basil	Salt and black pepper to taste
1 teaspoon dried oregano	

In a large skillet, heat olive oil on medium-low heat. Add garlic and blended onion, green pepper, and red pepper. Cook approximately 6 to 7 minutes, stirring occasionally. Add the basil, oregano, cumin, onion powder, and complete seasoning. Stir until well blended.

Add tomato puree and wine and heat thoroughly, approximately 3 to 4 minutes. Add this mixture to the black beans. Stir until well blended, cover, and continue to cook over low heat for about 45 minutes. Add salt and black pepper to taste.

Periodically check beans for water. Some beans, depending on the quality, absorb more liquid than others. Add water if needed. Also stir occasionally to avoid burning the beans, which may stick to the bottom of the soup pot. You can serve this as a soup or over white rice.   *8 servings*

GARBANZO BEAN SOUP

5 tablespoons olive oil
½ green bell pepper, blended
½ pound cooking ham, diced
1 pound soup beef, cut into small
    chunks
1 chorizo, sliced
6 ounces salt pork
1 teaspoon garlic powder

2 teaspoons onion powder
2 tablespoons Badia complete seasoning
8 cups water
1 pound potatoes, peeled and cut into
    chunks
½ pound cabbage
16-ounce can garbanzo beans

In a large soup pot, heat 5 tablespoons of olive oil over medium heat. Sauté blended green pepper, ham, beef, chorizo, and salt pork, stirring constantly for 2 to 3 minutes. Add the garlic powder, onion powder, and complete seasoning. Add water and bring to a boil. Add potatoes, cabbage, and garbanzo beans. Cook over medium heat until potatoes are tender.   *6 servings*

SPLIT PEA SOUP

6½ cups water
2 cups chicken broth
1 ham bone, containing approximately
    2 cups of meat
2 carrots, thinly sliced
1 medium onion, chopped
16 ounces split peas

1 tablespoon Badia complete seasoning
2 bay leaves
¼ teaspoon black pepper
1 small potato, peeled and cut into
    small chunks
Salt to taste

In a 5-quart pot, mix water, broth, bone, carrots, onion, and peas. Over medium heat, bring to a boil. Add complete seasoning, bay leaves, and black pepper. Reduce heat to low, cover, and simmer for 30 minutes.

Add potatoes and cook an additional 30 minutes, or until potatoes are tender. Remove bone, cut off meat, and return meat to soup for serving.

8 servings

NAVY BEAN SOUP

16-ounce package navy beans
8½ cups water
1 pound bacon, diced
2 large onions, diced
2 celery stalks, diced
4 chicken-flavor bouillon cubes

2 bay leaves
½ teaspoon salt
¼ teaspoon white pepper
1 tablespoon Badia complete seasoning
16-ounce can diced tomatoes

In a large saucepot, over high heat, heat beans and water to boiling. Boil for 3 minutes. Remove from heat and let stand covered for 1 hour.

Meanwhile in a 12-inch skillet, over medium heat, brown bacon, stirring frequently. Spoon off all fat, except ¼ cup. In same skillet with bacon and fat, cook onions and celery until tender, stirring frequently for about 10 minutes.

Stir bacon mixture into undrained beans. Add chicken-flavor bouillon cubes, bay leaves, salt, white pepper, and complete seasoning. Heat to boiling. Reduce heat to low; cover and simmer for 1½ hours.

When beans are tender, stir in tomatoes with their liquid. Cover and cook another 30 minutes, until beans are very tender and soup has thickened.

6 to 8 servings

SOPA DE CEBOLLA (ONION SOUP)

2 cups onions, thinly sliced
4 tablespoons butter
1½ cups beef consommé
1 cup water

½ teaspoon Worcestershire sauce
1 laurel leaf
4 slices toasted bread
½ cup shredded Parmesan cheese

Over low heat, cook the onions in butter until soft. Add the consommé, water, Worcestershire sauce, and laurel leaf. Cook over low heat for 25 minutes.

Cut the toasted bread in cubes and place in 4 individual oven-safe soup bowls. Pour the soup mixture over the bread. Add the Parmesan cheese on top. Place in the oven, and broil until cheese is melted and light brown.   *4 servings*

VICHYSSOISE

3 medium leeks

4 tablespoons butter

3 medium potatoes, peeled and thinly
   sliced

3 cups water

2 chicken-flavor bouillon cubes

1 cup heavy cream

1 cup milk

1 teaspoon salt

¼ teaspoon white pepper

Sour cream for topping

Chives for garnish, fresh or dried

Use only the white part of the leeks, and rinse well with cold water. Cut the white part crosswise into ¼-inch slices to make 2 cups.

In a large saucepan, over medium heat, cook leeks for 5 minutes in hot butter. Add potatoes, water, and chicken-flavor bouillon cubes. Bring to a boil. Reduce heat to low, cover, and simmer for 30 minutes.

Put about ¼ of the leek and potato mixture in a blender and, at low speed, blend until smooth. Repeat this process until all the mixture is used. Pour into a large saucepan. Stir the remaining ingredients, except sour cream and chives, into the mixture. Over low heat, cook soup just until heated through.

Pour soup into a large bowl, cover, and refrigerate until chilled. Serve in individual bowls and garnish with sour cream and chives.   *8 servings*

CREAM OF CHEDDAR CHEESE SOUP

½ cup butter

1 onion, chopped

¼ cup all-purpose flour

3 cups chicken broth

3 cups milk or half-and-half

4 cups cheddar cheese, shredded

In a medium soup pot, over medium heat, melt butter and then add onion. Cook until tender, about 3 minutes. Stir in the flour and blend. Add chicken broth and stir until well blended and mixture begins to thicken. Add milk and heat to boiling, stirring frequently.

In a blender, put half of the mixture and blend until smooth. Repeat process until all of the mixture is blended and return to pot. Bring to a boil and remove from heat. Stir in cheddar cheese and continue to stir until cheese is melted. If needed, return to low heat and cook an additional minute.   *6 servings*

CHEDDAR CHEESE AND BROCCOLI SOUP

This is a favorite of mine, especially in the winter. My mom used to make it for us all the time, and it was a meal in itself. She would serve it with toasted Cuban bread drizzled with olive oil and salt.

The first time my dad saw a piece of broccoli, he looked at my mom and said, "*¿Que es eso?* [What is this?]"

"Broccoli," she said, "and you will like it." Having studied in the United States, she was more diversified in her eating habits than he was.

½ cup butter	*⅛ teaspoon black pepper*
1 onion, chopped	*2 cups milk or half-and-half*
¼ cup all-purpose flour	*14 ounces chicken broth*
½ teaspoon salt	*1 cup water*
¼ teaspoon oregano	*1½ pounds broccoli, chopped*
¼ teaspoon Badia complete seasoning	*1½ cups sharp cheddar cheese, shredded*

In a large soup pot, melt butter over medium heat. Add onions and cook until tender, about 6 to 8 minutes, stirring constantly.

Stir in flour, salt, oregano, complete seasoning, and black pepper. Gradually stir in milk, chicken broth, and 1 cup water. Add broccoli and bring to boil over high heat. Reduce heat to low, cover and simmer until broccoli is tender, about 12 to 15 minutes.

In a blender, put about ¼ of the broccoli mixture in the container and mix until smooth. Repeat process until all of broccoli mixture is smooth and return to pot. Add cheddar cheese to mixture and stir over low heat until cheese is melted. *6 servings*

AJIACO (CUBAN VEGETABLE SOUP)

¼ cup olive oil

1 pound skirt steak, cut into chunks

½ pound chicken meat, cut into chunks

½ pound fresh pork, cut into chunks

1 chorizo, sliced

¼ pound salted pork

1 large green bell pepper, finely chopped

1 large onion, finely chopped

3 garlic cloves, minced

16-ounce can tomato sauce

¼ cup dry wine

8 cups water

1 bay leaf

1 teaspoon cumin

1 teaspoon ground oregano

1 pound yuca, peeled and cut into chunks

1 green plantain, peeled and cut into chunks

½ pound malanga, cut into chunks

½ pound white sweet potato, cut into chunks

1 yellow plantain, peeled and cut into chunks

2 ears of corn, husks removed, cut into chunks

Salt and black pepper to taste

In a large soup pot, heat olive oil over medium-high heat. Sauté steak, chicken, pork, chorizo, and salted pork in heated oil. Add green pepper, onion, garlic, tomato sauce, and wine. Stirring occasionally, cook until meats are done, approximately 10 minutes.

Add water, bay leaf, cumin, and oregano. On medium heat, add vegetables in 3-minute intervals, in the order they are listed in the ingredients.

Bring to a boil and then simmer for approximately 20 to 25 minutes until roots and vegetables are fork-tender.

Add salt and black pepper to taste.

6 to 8 servings

BEEF VEGETABLE SOUP

¼ cup olive oil

1 small onion, diced

3 medium carrots, sliced

2 celery stalks, sliced

½ head cabbage, shredded

1¾ pounds stew beef, cubed

3 medium potatoes, peeled and cubed

3 malangas, peeled and cubed

28-ounce can tomatoes

16-ounce can corn, drained

6 cups water

2 teaspoons Badia complete seasoning

½ teaspoon dried basil

½ teaspoon black pepper

Salt to taste

To an 8-quart saucepot over high heat, add olive oil and cook onion, carrots, celery, and cabbage until lightly browned, stirring frequently. With a slotted spoon, remove vegetables, putting them aside.

In the same saucepot, over high heat, add chunks of beef and brown on all sides. Add reserved vegetables, potatoes, malangas, tomatoes with liquid, corn, water, and all other remaining ingredients and bring to a boil. Reduce heat to low, cover, and simmer for 40 minutes or until beef and potatoes are tender.

8 servings

CALDO BASICO (BEEF CONSOMMÉ)

1 pound beef

1½ pounds beef bones

1 onion, peeled and halved

1 green bell pepper, cleaned and halved

6 garlic cloves

1 laurel leaf

½ bunch fresh parsley

4 cilantro leaves

2 teaspoons salt

¼ cup ground cumin

1 pinch saffron

2 fresh carrots, sliced

12 cups water

Place all ingredients in a large pot. Cook at moderate heat until the liquid breaks into a boil. Reduce heat and cook until half the liquid is reduced, approximately 2 hours.

When cool, drain the liquid for broth.

6 servings

RABO ENCENDIDO
(OXTAIL STEW)

5 pounds oxtails, cut into 2-inch chunks
1 cup flour
¼ cup olive oil
1 cup beef broth
1 cup red wine
¼ cup tomato paste mixed with 2 cups
   water
1 bay leaf
½ teaspoon dried basil

½ teaspoon dried oregano
¼ teaspoon cumin
1 teaspoon Badia complete seasoning
2 onions, chopped
2 green bell peppers, seeded and
   coarsely chopped
2 garlic cloves, minced
Parsley for garnish

Trim excess fat from oxtails. Lightly cover the oxtails in flour. Heat olive oil in a large saucepot over medium-high heat and brown oxtails for about 2 to 3 minutes.

Add beef broth, wine, tomato paste mixture, and all other ingredients, except parsley. Bring to a boil, cover, and simmer for 2½ to 3 hours. Add more broth or water as necessary while simmering. Transfer stew to a serving platter and garnish.   *6 servings*

OYSTER STEW

2 medium leeks, sliced (about ⅔ cup)
3 tablespoons butter
3 tablespoons all-purpose flour
1 teaspoon anchovy paste
1 tablespoon Badia complete seasoning

2 cups half-and-half
2 cups milk
6 cups shucked, clean oysters
   (about 3 pints)

In a 4-quart pot, cook leeks in butter until tender. Stir in flour, anchovy paste, and complete seasoning until well mixed. Add half-and-half and milk, stirring occasionally until slightly thickened and bubbly.

Drain oysters and reserve 3 cups liquid. In a large saucepan, combine reserved liquid and oysters. Cover and cook a few minutes until oysters curl at the edges. Skim surface of the liquid. Add oysters and liquid into cream mixture. For a thicker stew, do not add all of the liquid to the cream mixture. *8 servings*

SHRIMP BISQUE

1½ pounds medium shrimp, shelled and deveined, reserve shells
4 tablespoons olive oil
4 tablespoons butter
1 large onion, chopped
1 carrot, chopped
1 celery stalk, chopped
3 chicken-flavor bouillon cubes
2½ cups water

1 cup chablis
¼ cup long grain rice
1 bay leaf
½ teaspoon Badia complete seasoning
¼ teaspoon cayenne pepper
Salt to taste
16-ounce can tomatoes
2 cups heavy cream

In a large soup pot, over medium heat, cook shrimp shells in hot olive oil until pink, stirring constantly. Discard shells, leaving the oil in the pot.

Add shrimp to oil and cook over medium heat, stirring frequently, until shrimp turn pink, approximately 3 minutes. Remove shrimp from pot and set aside.

Still on medium heat, add butter, onion, carrot, and celery. Cook, stirring occasionally, until tender.

Dilute the chicken-flavor bouillon cubes in the 2½ cups water and add to pot. Add the wine, rice, bay leaf, complete seasoning, cayenne pepper, and salt. Bring to a boil. Reduce heat to low, cover, and simmer for 20 minutes or until rice is tender.

Remove pot from heat, and discard bay leaf. Drain juice from tomatoes into rice mixture. Remove seeds from tomatoes and stir tomatoes into rice mixture. Add cooked shrimp.

Put half the mixture into a blender, and blend until smooth. Add the other half. Return shrimp mixture to pot, stir in cream and bring to a boil over medium heat.

Remove from heat and serve.   *6 to 8 servings*

GAZPACHO

4 tablespoons olive oil

3 cups tomato juice

1 small onion, chopped

1 cucumber, peeled and seeded

3 large tomatoes, peeled and seeded

½ green bell pepper

1 garlic clove

¾ teaspoon salt

½ teaspoon hot pepper sauce

In a blender, on high speed, blend all ingredients, ⅓ at a time, until smooth. Pour into large bowl, cover, and chill before serving.   *4 servings*

The next two soups are great for hot summer days out by the pool. They are not only refreshing but are easy to make.

STRAWBERRY SOUP

1 pint strawberries, hulled

½ cup chablis

1 teaspoon grated lemon peel

½ cup sugar

2 tablespoons lemon juice

In a covered blender, on medium speed, blend strawberries and all other ingredients until smooth. Refrigerate until cold. Serve soup in chilled bowls. You may garnish with edible flowers, orange peel, or even strawberries with lemon peels.   *3 servings*

BLUEBERRY SOUP

⅓ cup sour cream

2 tablespoons sugar, or to taste

2 10-ounce packages frozen blueberries, partially thawed

In a covered blender, at low speed, blend sour cream, blueberries and sugar until smooth. Refrigerate until ready for use. Serve soup in chilled bowls and garnish with edible flowers, lime slices, or strawberries.   *2 servings*

ENSALADAS

SALADS

In Cuba, tossed green salads were unusual. The most popular salads consisted of watercress, iceberg lettuce, tomatoes, and avocados. My dad was not a big fan of salads, but he loved avocados. My mom and I, however, loved salads. We commonly used endive, watercress, avocados, and the many types of tomatoes available. Mima likes beefsteaks, and I prefer plum or grape tomatoes. The dressings are very simple, usually a vinaigrette, olive oil with lemon juice, and a sprinkle of kosher salt and black pepper, or just an Italian dressing. At Habana Café, I do a Spanish salad that is not traditional Cuban cuisine, but very popular. The feta and Parmesan cheeses add great flavor. When I cater, I add other ingredients, as you will see. Salads are great appetizers or can be used as a main dish.

SPANISH SALAD

1 head iceberg lettuce, washed
3 tomatoes, sliced or diced
1 cucumber, peeled and thinly sliced
Green or black olives, as many as you like

¼ cup feta cheese
¼ cup Parmesan cheese
½ teaspoon dried basil

In a salad bowl, tear iceberg lettuce into bite-sized pieces. Add tomatoes, cucumbers, olives, feta cheese, Parmesan cheese, and basil. Lightly toss to mix ingredients well. Then add Italian dressing, or a dressing of your choice, and toss again until the dressing coats the salad. Serve on chilled salad plates.

6 servings

SPANISH SALAD (CATERING VERSION)

1-pound bag garden salad
1 pint grape tomatoes, halved lengthwise
1 14-ounce can salad-cut hearts of
    palm, drained
1 13.75-ounce can artichokes, drained
    and cut into quarters

1 can black olives, drained
1 15-ounce can asparagus spears,
    drained
8 ounces feta cheese, crumbled
6 ounces Parmesan cheese
1 tablespoon dried basil

In a large salad bowl, combine all ingredients, add dressing to taste, and lightly toss until all ingredients are coated. Serve on chilled salad plates. *8 servings*

CAESAR SALAD

2 medium heads romaine lettuce,
    washed and torn into bite-sized pieces
⅓ cup olive oil
2 tablespoons lemon juice
Salt and black pepper to taste

¼ teaspoon anchovy paste
⅓ cup grated Parmesan cheese
2-ounce can anchovy fillets, drained
1 box garlic croutons

Put lettuce into a salad bowl. In a separate bowl, add olive oil, lemon juice, salt, black pepper, and anchovy paste, and whisk together. Add Parmesan cheese and anchovies to lettuce, then pour dressing mixture over that and toss until lettuce is coated. Before serving, add croutons. *6 servings*

WATERCRESS AND ENDIVE SALAD

¾ pound endive
2 bunches watercress
Kosher salt to taste

Black pepper to taste
1 lemon, juiced
¼ cup olive oil

Trim bottoms of endive and separate leaves, putting them in a salad bowl. Cut watercress bunches into thirds. Toss together. Add salt, black pepper, lemon juice, and olive oil to taste. Toss until salad is well coated. *4 to 6 servings*

AVOCADO SALAD

3 large avocados, pitted, halved
   lengthwise, and thinly sliced
1 red onion, cut in half, and thinly
   sliced

Salt and black pepper to taste
½ cup olive oil
3 tablespoons red vinegar
Parsley for garnish

On a serving platter, arrange the avocado slices and place the thin slices of on-ion on top of the avocado. Sprinkle with salt and black pepper. Whisk olive oil and vinegar together and pour over salad. Garnish with parsley.   *6 servings*

SLICED TOMATO AND MOZZARELLA CHEESE WITH FRESH BASIL

2 tablespoons olive oil
1½ tablespoons lemon juice
¼ teaspoon salt, or to taste
¼ teaspoon black pepper, or
   to taste

4 large beefsteak tomatoes, cut into
   ½-inch slices
8 ounces fresh mozzarella cheese,
   cut ¼-inch thick
14 fresh basil leaves

Mix olive oil, lemon juice, salt, and black pepper. Arrange tomatoes, cheese, and basil alternately on a large serving platter and coat with dressing.   *8 servings*

VINAIGRETTE

1 cup olive oil
4 tablespoons wine vinegar
2 tablespoons lemon juice
1 garlic clove, minced

1 tablespoon dried basil
1 tablespoon dried oregano
Salt and black pepper to taste
1 tablespoon Dijon mustard

Mix all ingredients in a jar and shake until well blended. Refrigerate until ready for use.   *Yield 1½ cups*

CHICKEN SALAD

2 2½-pound chickens
¼ cup chablis
1 tablespoon Badia complete seasoning
1 tablespoon ground cumin
1 tablespoon ground laurel
1 tablespoon ground oregano
1 tablespoon garlic powder
2 pounds red potatoes, boiled and cut
    into small pieces

½ cup celery, finely chopped
½ cup stuffed green olives, halved
1 large apple, peeled and diced
1½ cups mayonnaise

For garnish:
¼ cup canned, chopped pimentos
1 can small early peas
2 hard-boiled eggs, cut in quarters

Season chickens with white wine and dry ingredients and marinate overnight.

Preheat oven to 350°F. Remove chickens from marinade and bake for approximately 1½ hours or until done. Let stand and cool.

When cool, remove chicken skins and debone. Cut into small cubes.

Mix meat with the potatoes, celery, olives, and diced apples. Fold in mayonnaise. Refrigerate for 2 hours.

Before serving, garnish with pimentos, peas, and eggs.   *8 servings*

⮜ PLATOS PRINCIPALES ⮞

MAIN DISHES

Dinner parties at home are my favorite form of entertaining. Maybe it is because they remind me so much of my childhood and all the great stories I got to hear that I otherwise might not have known.

When I was growing up, everybody seemed to help in the kitchen, and my mom and her sisters would divide up the different courses. One sister would be preparing the salads, while the others did the main dish, desserts, drinks, and coffee. Looking back, now that I have my own kitchen experiences, I realize that they all knew what they were good at and stuck to it. It never seemed to get too complicated that way.

My aunt Alina was more than happy to share a few of her favorite recipes for this book. We started talking about cooking and one thing led to another, and she talked about the old Cuba, how spectacular it was, and then the awful contrast with her arrival in the United States.

The revolution was just a year old when parents got their first scare. The Education Ministry announced a new military program for high school students. All children had to learn to bear arms. They were also instructed at the schools to inform on their parents and neighbors. Indoctrination became a constant in schools, on the radio, and on television. The panic among parents was rampant. They started sending their children alone out of the country. Rumors circulated that the government was going to take over legal guardianship of children. The state wanted to guide their education, provide living accommodations, and send them abroad to study behind the Iron Curtain. In January 1961, the first one thousand students departed for the Soviet Union. Eight months later, in September, thousands of families were desperately trying to send their children out of the country. Flights began arriving daily in Miami with as many as sixty children without their parents. In January 1962 the U.S. State Department granted the Catholic Welfare Bureau the authority to provide a visa waiver to children between the ages of six and sixteen who wished to enter the United States under the guardianship of the Catholic Diocese of Miami. Thus began Operation Peter Pan. Within four months, in May of 1962, it was reported that ten thousand unaccompanied children had arrived in the United States with another five hundred arriving each month.

In October 1962 the Cuban Missile Crisis brought Operation Peter Pan to an end. It has been estimated that approximately fourteen thousand children entered the United States from Cuba. Left behind were over fifty thousand children who had received visas, but did not get out in time. Aunt Alina went to a foster home in Chippewa Falls, Wisconsin, in 1962 at the age of sixteen. She finished high school there and went on to get a degree in dietetics from Viterbo College in La Crosse, Wisconsin.

Aunt Alina loves to cook, and you will find her recipes throughout this book, such as the Fillet of Fish Breaded in Plantain Chips, her Paella, Moros y Cristianos (Black Beans and Rice), Arroz Relleno (Stuffed Rice), and the Arroz con Leche (Rice Pudding) and Mango Cheesecake.

FILLET OF FISH BREADED IN PLANTAIN CHIPS

At Habana Café, I use either catfish or grouper for this recipe. Customers love this batter because it is unusual and gives the fish a very exotic taste.

6 eggs
4 teaspoons Badia complete
  seasoning
4 pieces fish

1 6-ounce bag plantain chips, processed
  in a food processor
Vegetable oil for frying
Lime wedges for garnish

In a large bowl, whisk eggs and complete seasoning until well mixed. Take fish and place in egg mixture. Make sure fish is coated on both sides.

On a piece of waxed paper, spread out plantain crumbs. Take fish and lightly press in plantain crumbs until they stick to fish on both sides.

In a 12-inch skillet, pour about 3 inches of vegetable oil and heat on high. Reduce heat to medium-high, and fry fish until golden brown. Cooking time will depend on the thickness of your fillets. Garnish with lime.   *4 servings*

BACALAO A LA VIZCAÍNA (CODFISH)

This was one of the most popular fish dishes in Cuba. Its origin is Spanish, and once you taste cod prepared like this, you will have a new appreciation for this usually very salty fish.

1 pound codfish	*¼ teaspoon cumin*
1 tablespoon oil	*¼ teaspoon ground oregano*
1 pound potatoes, peeled and sliced	*¼ teaspoon black pepper*
into ¼-inch rounds	*¼ teaspoon ground laurel*
1 medium green bell pepper, thinly	*⅓ cup water*
sliced	*⅓ cup chablis*
1 large onion, peeled and thinly sliced	*1 teaspoon vinegar*
4 garlic cloves, minced	*½ cup tomato sauce*
⅓ cup olive oil	*6-ounce can pimentos, chopped*

If not using fresh cod, place fish in a large pot and cover with cold water. Change water once after 3 to 4 hours, soaking the cod for at least 12 hours before cooking. Drain, remove any bones and skin, and cut fish into 4-inch pieces.

Place cod in a large pot. Cover with water and bring to a boil over high heat. Lower the heat until fish is tender, about 30 minutes. Drain fish and set aside.

Coat the bottom of a large skillet with 1 tablespoon of oil. Place the potato slices in the skillet, covering the bottom completely. Layer the codfish on top of the potato slices and then layer green pepper and onion on top of the fish.

In a bowl, mix the remaining ingredients and pour over the fish mixture. Bring contents of the skillet to a boil, reduce heat to low, cover, and simmer for about 1 hour or until the potatoes are tender. This dish is traditionally served over a bed of white rice.   *6 servings*

FILETES DE PARGO CON ALMENDRAS
(RED SNAPPER WITH ALMONDS)

1 pound red snapper fillets
2 garlic cloves, minced
1 teaspoon salt
⅛ teaspoon cumin
1 lemon or lime, juiced
⅛ teaspoon black pepper
1 cup flour
1 cup butter
¼ cup fresh parsley, finely chopped

For the sauce:
2 tablespoons flour
½ cup dry wine
½ cup melted butter
1 medium onion, minced
½ cup toasted almonds, finely chopped
Parsley for garnish

Marinate fish with minced garlic, salt, cumin, lemon juice, and black pepper. Dip in flour and sauté in hot butter until done. When finished, reserve ½ cup of the hot butter.

For the sauce, dissolve flour in wine. In the reserved butter, sauté the minced onion, add the flour mixture, and allow to thicken. Add the chopped almonds and cover fish with sauce. Sprinkle parsley on top. *4 servings*

SALMON WITH MANGO SALSA

I use this mango salsa every time I grill salmon. The salmon, with its rich nuances in flavor and texture, pairs well with the juicy and exotically sweet mango.

For salsa:
1 cup ripe mango, peeled and chopped
¼ cup red onion, finely chopped
2 tablespoons fresh cilantro, chopped
1 tablespoon fresh mint, chopped
3 tablespoons orange juice
1 jalapeño pepper, seeded and minced

¼ teaspoon salt
¼ teaspoon cumin

For salmon:
4 12-ounce salmon fillets
¼ teaspoon salt
1 tablespoon blackened seasoning

Combine all salsa ingredients. Mix well and chill for 30 minutes.

Sprinkle fillets with salt and blackened seasoning. Coat a large skillet with vegetable cooking spray and cook fillets, over medium heat, for 6 minutes on each side, or until done.

Serve immediately with mango salsa.   *4 servings*

LOBSTER THERMIDOR

4 1½-pound lobsters, cooked
6 tablespoons butter
3 tablespoons all-purpose flour
½ teaspoon salt
⅛ teaspoon ground nutmeg
⅛ teaspoon paprika

¼ teaspoon Badia complete seasoning
1½ cups half-and-half
4 tablespoons sherry
½ cup shredded sharp cheddar cheese
Chopped parsley for garnish

Remove all lobster meat, the roe, and the liver, but leave the shell whole from the tail to the head. Do not twist head from tail. Wash shell and drain. Put on tray and refrigerate.

Cut lobster meat into small chunks and put in a bowl along with roe and liver. Cover and refrigerate.

About 30 minutes before you are ready to serve, in a medium saucepan, over medium heat, add butter until it foams and then add flour, salt, nutmeg, paprika, and complete seasoning. Stir, and then add half-and-half and sherry. Stir until mixture thickens. Add lobster and cook until heated through, stirring occasionally.

Preheat broiler. Fill shells with mixture and sprinkle with cheddar cheese. Broil until cheese has melted. When ready to serve, garnish with chopped parsley.   *4 servings*

SHRIMP AJILLO

1½ cups butter

2 tablespoons garlic, minced

3 tablespoons parsley, chopped

⅛ teaspoon salt

½ teaspoon lemon juice

2 pounds medium shrimp, shelled
   and deveined

¼ cup chablis

In a 12-inch skillet, melt butter. When butter is foamy, add garlic, parsley, salt, and lemon juice and stir. Add shrimp and white wine and cook about 5 minutes, or until shrimp turn pink in color. If you need more butter, add some. Butter should be creamy when serving, and butter can separate rather quickly.

Transfer shrimp to serving bowl and garnish with parsley. This dish is great over pasta.

4 to 6 servings

CAMARONES ENCHILADOS (SHRIMP CREOLE)

This is very popular at the restaurant. It has a bit of a kick to it because of the hot sauce. Usually, Cuban food is not spicy hot. A lot of customers who come to the restaurant for the first time say, "Nothing too hot." I always tell them, "This is Cuban, not Mexican." It is amazing to me how Mexican and Cuban food are so easily confused. The two are actually very different. Mexican food uses a great deal of chili peppers, while Cuban food uses green and red bell peppers and the food is not overly spicy. For this dish, all you need is a bed of fluffy white rice to go with it.

½ cup olive oil

1 medium onion, finely chopped

3 garlic cloves, finely chopped

1 large green bell pepper, finely chopped

8 ounces canned tomato sauce

8 ounces canned, chopped pimentos

½ cup tomato ketchup

½ cup dry wine

1 teaspoon vinegar

1 teaspoon Worcestershire sauce

1 teaspoon Tabasco hot sauce

1 bay leaf

1½ teaspoons salt

1 teaspoon black pepper

½ teaspoon cumin

½ teaspoon oregano

2 pounds shrimp, cleaned and deveined

½ cup fresh parsley, finely chopped

In a medium pot, heat oil and sauté onions, garlic, and bell pepper for approximately 10 minutes. Add tomato sauce, pimentos, ketchup, wine, vinegar, Worcestershire sauce, hot sauce, and remaining dry ingredients. Cover and cook over medium heat for 15 to 20 minutes. Stir occasionally.

While the sauce is cooking, sauté shrimp in a skillet with a small amount of oil, for approximately 5 minutes. Add shrimp to the tomato sauce. Add parsley. Simmer for approximately 10 minutes. *6 servings*

SEAFOOD GUMBO

This Creole specialty is a favorite of mine. In addition to being a restaurant owner, I am also a flight attendant. Any time I lay over in New Orleans, this is the only thing I eat. No matter where I get it, it is always good. I brought some home with me so I could try to duplicate it. Through trial and error I came up with the following recipe.

¼ cup all-purpose flour	2 16-ounce cans tomatoes
¼ cup olive oil	10 ounces frozen okra, sliced
1 green bell pepper, diced	6 cups water
1 large onion, diced	1 pound shrimp, shelled and deveined
3 garlic cloves, minced	½ pound fresh Alaska king crab (or
1 teaspoon thyme leaves	substitute a 6-ounce frozen package)
3 teaspoons salt	¼ teaspoon hot pepper sauce
1 dozen oysters in shells	8 servings of hot, cooked rice

In a large soup pot, over medium heat, stir flour constantly in very hot olive oil until dark brown, approximately 6 to 7 minutes. Do not burn.

Stir in green pepper, onion, garlic, thyme, and salt. Cook until onion and pepper are tender, stirring frequently.

Open oysters and drain their liquid into flour mixture. Refrigerate oysters.

Add tomatoes with their liquid, okra, and water to the pot. Bring to a boil. Reduce heat to low and simmer for 30 minutes or until mixture is slightly thickened.

Add the oysters, shrimp, crab, and hot pepper sauce. Cook about 8 to 10 minutes or until shrimp are done. They will look pink.

Serve in bowls with a scoop of hot rice. *8 servings*

ARROZ CON CALAMARES
(RICE WITH SQUID)

2 teaspoons olive oil

1 large onion, chopped

1 large green bell pepper, finely chopped

3 garlic cloves, finely chopped

1 can pimentos, cut into strips, reserve liquid

2 cans squid (approximately 113 grams)

½ cup dry wine

2 bay leaves

1 teaspoon salt

¼ teaspoon black pepper

½ teaspoon cumin

1 pound long grain rice

2½ cups water

1 can green sweet peas

In a saucepan, heat oil and sauté the onion, green pepper, garlic, pimentos, and reserved pimento liquid.

Add squid with the juice. Cook for approximately 5 minutes, stirring frequently. Add dry wine, bay leaves, salt, black pepper, and cumin. Cook for an additional 2 minutes.

Add rice and water. Bring to a boil and immediately simmer at medium heat until the rice is cooked, approximately 25 to 30 minutes. Garnish with green sweet peas.

6 servings

PICADILLO

Picadillo is always served over a bed of white rice. Sweet plantains are great with this dish.

¼ cup olive oil

1 red bell pepper, blended

¼ cup capers

¼ cup green olives

2 tablespoons Badia complete seasoning

1 packet Knorr all-purpose seasoning

1 cup tomato puree

1 cup chablis

1 teaspoon vinegar

Salt and black pepper to taste

½ teaspoon cumin

1 small onion, minced

3 garlic cloves, minced

2 pounds lean ground beef

1 cup early peas

¼ cup raisins

1 cup potatoes, cubed

In a large saucepan, heat olive oil over medium heat. When hot, add all ingredients except ground beef, peas, raisins, and potatoes. Sauté this until hot.

Reduce heat to medium and add ground beef. Stir occasionally. Cover and cook about 20 minutes, then add peas, raisins, and potatoes, and cook uncovered for another 20 minutes to reduce sauce.

6 to 8 servings

ROPA VIEJA
(OLD CLOTHES)

This dish got its name from the meat, which was first used to make beef broth and then "handed down" to this dish like hand-me-down clothes.

4 pounds flank steak
1 cup beef broth reserved from boiling
* process*
½ cup olive oil
1 cup tomato puree
1 teaspoon onion powder
1 tablespoon garlic, minced
1 tablespoon Badia complete seasoning
½ cup red pimentos

1 medium green bell pepper, cut into
* strips*
1 medium red bell pepper, cut into
* strips*
1 cup chablis
2 bay leaves
1 medium onion, thinly sliced
Salt and black pepper to taste
Cornstarch (optional)

Boil flank steak for 2 hours and remove, reserving 1 cup broth. Let meat cool, then shred by hand into strips. Set meat aside. In a large saucepan, heat oil, add broth and all remaining ingredients together, and cook over medium heat for 15 to 20 minutes. Stir in beef and simmer for 20 minutes. If sauce seems too thick, add a little more broth; if too thin, add 1 teaspoon of cornstarch dissolved in cold water. Serve over a bed of white rice.

6 to 8 servings

PALOMILLA STEAK

This is a very popular dish at the restaurant. The best way to serve this is with white rice, black beans, and either fried sweet plantains or tostones, which are green plantains.

6 7-ounce top round steaks, pounded
   to ½-inch thick
2 garlic cloves, minced
1 teaspoon salt

2 tablespoons butter or margarine
2 limes
½ medium onion, finely chopped
½ bunch parsley, finely chopped

Rub steaks with garlic and sprinkle with salt. In a large skillet, melt butter or margarine over medium heat. Begin frying steaks 1 or 2 at a time, depending on the size of your skillet. Because the steaks are so thin, cook them for about 3 minutes on each side.

Place steaks on a plate, squeeze lime juice over them, and garnish with raw chopped onion and parsley.

6 servings

STEAK DIANE

4 rib-eye steaks, ½-inch thick
Salt and black pepper to taste
½ teaspoon Badia complete seasoning
4 tablespoons butter

4 tablespoons brandy
3 small shallots, chopped
3 tablespoons chives, chopped
½ cup sherry

On a cutting board, pound steaks with a meat mallet to ¼-inch thickness. Sprinkle each side with salt, black pepper, and complete seasoning.

In a 12-inch skillet, over medium-high heat, melt 1 tablespoon butter and cook steaks 1 at a time until both sides are browned. Pour 1 tablespoon brandy over each steak, and with a match or small propane torch, set aflame.

As flaming stops with each steak, stir in ¼ of the shallots and ¼ of the chives, stirring constantly until shallots are tender, about 1 minute. Add 2 tablespoons of sherry and heat through. Keep steaks warm in oven at 200°F until each is cooked. Place steaks on a warm dinner plate, pour mixture over them, and serve.

4 servings

HIGADO A LA ITALIANA
(SAUTÉED LIVER, ITALIAN STYLE)

1½ pounds beef liver

¼ teaspoon oregano powder

Salt and black pepper to taste

6 garlic cloves, minced

¼ cup vinegar

½ pound onions, sliced

5 medium green bell peppers, sliced

½ cup olive oil

Cut the liver into medium slices. Season with oregano, salt, black pepper, minced garlic, and vinegar.

Top with onion slices and green pepper strips. Marinate for 3 to 4 hours.

Remove liver from marinade and, in hot oil, sauté liver, continuously stirring until cooked. Serve immediately.   *6 to 8 servings*

POT ROAST

5-pound bottom-round roast, rinsed

2 garlic cloves, minced

¼ cup all-purpose flour

¼ cup salad oil

1 cup tomato sauce

¼ cup olive oil

2 tablespoons Badia complete seasoning

2 medium carrots, sliced

2 medium onions, chopped

1 cup celery, thinly sliced

1 teaspoon salt

1 teaspoon black pepper

1 tablespoon oregano

Parsley for garnish

Rub garlic all over meat. On waxed paper, lightly coat roast with flour.

In large saucepan, over high heat, sear roast in hot salad oil until evenly browned on all sides.

Add tomato sauce and all remaining ingredients except parsley. Heat to boiling, and reduce heat to low. Cover and simmer for 4 hours or until meat is fork-tender. Turn roast over occasionally. Adjust seasoning if needed. Transfer meat to a warm platter.

Fill blender with liquid and vegetables and blend at high speed. Pour into saucepot and repeat process until all vegetables are blended. Heat mixture to boiling and pour over roast. Garnish with parsley.   *10 servings*

BOLICHE
(STUFFED POT ROAST)

This is a very traditional Cuban dish. You can buy the eye of round in all Cuban markets, already stuffed with chorizo or ham. I prefer chorizo, because it is a lot more flavorful than ham. If you live in an area where there is not a Cuban market, you can stuff the roast yourself. When you buy the eye of round, ask the butcher to cut a pocket through the center of the roast. It should be cut 1½ inches straight through the center, end to end.

4-pound eye of round, rinsed
chorizo, enough to fill the center
  lengthwise
½ cup olive oil
2 large onions, sliced
6 garlic cloves, minced
1 cup chablis
2 teaspoons dried oregano
2 teaspoons dried basil

2 teaspoons onion powder
2 tablespoons Badia complete seasoning
1 teaspoon cumin
1 teaspoon black pepper
½ cup pimentos
Salt, to taste
3 cups beef broth
1½ cups tomato puree

Starting at either end of the roast, stuff the chorizo all the way through.

In a very large saucepan, big enough for the entire roast, add olive oil and heat over medium heat. Add onions and minced garlic. Stir frequently, until onions are transparent.

Add ½ cup chablis, stir, and add oregano, basil, onion powder, complete seasoning, cumin, black pepper, and pimentos.

Place roast in the pot and add the remaining chablis. Cook meat about 5 minutes and turn. Taste liquid and adjust salt and other seasonings.

Mix beef broth and tomato puree and add that mixture to the pot. Bring to a boil.

Preheat oven to 350°F. Cover pot, and cook in oven for 2 hours. Remove from oven, let stand 10 minutes, and cut in ½-inch slices.

Mix the sauce well and serve over the roast. This is great with white rice, black beans, and sweet plantains.   *6 servings*

BOLICHE A LA NARANJADA
(POT ROAST WITH ORANGE SAUCE)

3 pounds eye of round
6 prunes, pitted
⅛ pound ham, diced
3 garlic cloves, minced
¼ teaspoon black pepper
¼ teaspoon ground laurel
¼ teaspoon ground cumin

1 teaspoon salt
1 cup dry white wine, divided in half
1 onion, sliced
1 green bell pepper, sliced
2 bacon strips
Salt to taste
2 cups orange juice

Using a sharp knife, make 6 1½-inch cuts to the meat. Fill the cuts with the prunes and the ham.

Season the meat with 2 garlic cloves, black pepper, laurel, cumin, salt, and ½ cup wine. Add sliced onion and green bell pepper. Leave to marinate for approximately 3 hours.

In a pot, cook the bacon strips, add the meat, and sauté in the bacon fat until golden brown.

When browned, add the additional garlic clove, salt to taste, ½ cup wine, and orange juice. Cover tightly and cook slowly until meat is tender, adding more orange juice and wine as necessary.   *8 servings*

CARNE CON PAPA (BEEF STEW WITH POTATOES)

2 pounds stew meat, in 2-inch cubes
3 garlic cloves, finely chopped
3 teaspoons salt
¼ teaspoon black pepper
¼ teaspoon cumin
¼ teaspoon oregano
1 bay leaf
½ cup dry wine

2 teaspoons vinegar
½ cup olive oil
1 large onion, chopped
1 green bell pepper, chopped
8 ounces tomato sauce
1 cup beef broth
2 medium red potatoes, quartered
½ cup chopped pimentos

Marinate stew meat in garlic, salt, black pepper, cumin, oregano, and bay leaf. Add dry wine and vinegar, cover, and refrigerate for 2 hours.

In a saucepan, heat oil and brown the stew meat. Add the onion, green pepper, tomato sauce, and beef broth. Cover, and cook over medium heat for approximately 1 hour, or until meat is tender.

Add potatoes and pimentos. Cook over low heat until potatoes are done, approximately 30 to 40 minutes. Add more beef broth if necessary.   *6 servings*

ALBONDIGAS (MEATBALLS)

1 pound ground beef
½ pound ground ham
1 teaspoon onion powder
1 teaspoon garlic powder
2 eggs
¼ cup milk or cream
1 cup cracker meal
1 teaspoon mustard
½ teaspoon salt
⅛ teaspoon black pepper
¼ teaspoon cumin
¼ teaspoon ground oregano
¼ teaspoon ground laurel
1 cup all-purpose flour

½ cup vegetable oil

For sauce:
¼ cup olive oil
1 onion, chopped
1 green bell pepper, chopped
2 garlic cloves, chopped
8 ounces tomato sauce
½ cup parsley, finely chopped
⅓ cup ketchup
1 teaspoon salt
1 teaspoon sugar
½ cup dry wine
½ cup canned pimentos, chopped

Mix together the first 13 ingredients and shape into round balls. Roll in flour and sauté in hot oil until golden brown. Drain the meatballs when brown.

To make the sauce, in the olive oil, sauté onion, green pepper, and garlic. Add the remaining sauce ingredients and cook for approximately 5 minutes. Add the meatballs to the sauce and cook slowly for 30 minutes. *8 servings*

VEAL STEW

I particularly like this dish served over pasta. Sweet plantains or tostones are just an added touch for a side dish.

1½ pounds veal steak, cut into chunks	*1 cup sherry*
2 tablespoons flour	*1 teaspoon Badia complete seasoning*
4 tablespoons olive oil	*Salt and white pepper to taste*
1 small onion, peeled and diced	*1½ pounds mushrooms, sliced*
1 cup water	*Chopped parsley for garnish*

Dip the veal chunks into the flour. In a large saucepan, heat olive oil, add meat, and brown on all sides. Remove.

Sauté the onion and, if necessary, add a little more olive oil. Return meat to pot and add water, sherry, and complete seasoning. Bring to a boil. Add salt and white pepper and reduce heat. Cover and simmer for 45 minutes or until meat is fork-tender.

Add mushrooms and a little more liquid if necessary, and cook another 30 minutes. Adjust seasonings if needed. If you have to thicken the sauce, do so with cornstarch diluted in cold water. Add to sauce and stir. Garnish with parsley. *4 servings*

VEAL MARSALA

2 tablespoons all-purpose flour
½ teaspoon salt
¼ teaspoon white pepper
¼ teaspoon Badia complete seasoning
4 veal shoulder-blade steaks, about
    ¾-inch thick

4 tablespoons butter
½ cup marsala wine
½ cup water
¼ pound mushrooms, sliced

In a small bowl, mix flour, salt, white pepper, and complete seasoning. On waxed paper, coat veal with flour mixture.

In a 12-inch skillet, over medium heat, add 4 tablespoons butter until foaming. Add veal. Cook on both sides until browned. Add more butter if needed. Remove veal onto a plate and keep warm. You can hold it in the oven at 200°F.

Reduce skillet heat to low. Stir in ½ cup marsala and ½ cup water to drippings, scraping to loosen brown bits. Return veal to skillet. Cover and allow to simmer. About 30 minutes into simmering, add mushrooms. Cover and cook for another 15 minutes, or until veal is tender.   *4 servings*

AJIES RELLENOS
(STUFFED PEPPERS)

½ pound ground beef
½ pound ground pork
½ pound ground ham
4 garlic cloves, finely chopped
1 large onion, finely chopped
1 teaspoon salt
½ teaspoon black pepper
1 teaspoon cumin
2 tablespoons olive oil
1 teaspoon vinegar

1 tablespoon dry wine
10 small stuffed olives, cut up
1 cup tomato sauce
2 cups cooked rice
2 eggs, well beaten
1 teaspoon flour
6 medium green bell peppers, cored
    and seeded
2 tablespoons cracker meal
2 tablespoons shredded Parmesan cheese

Mix the three meats together. Season meat mixture with garlic, onion, salt, black pepper, and cumin. Refrigerate for 30 minutes.

Heat oil and sauté meat mixture over medium heat. Add vinegar, wine, olives, tomato sauce, and rice, and cook for approximately 5 minutes, stirring constantly.

Remove from heat and add eggs and flour.

Stuff green peppers with the mixture. Sprinkle with cracker meal and Parmesan cheese. Bake at 375°F. for approximately 40 to 45 minutes.

6 servings

LAMB STEW

1 tablespoon olive oil	*1 tablespoon Badia complete seasoning*
2 pounds stew lamb, cut into 1½-inch	*¼ teaspoon rosemary, crushed*
chunks	*1 pint grape tomatoes*
1 cup blush wine	*3-ounce jar pimento-stuffed olives,*
2 garlic cloves, minced	*drained*
1 teaspoon salt	*6 servings cooked white rice*
¼ teaspoon black pepper	

In a 12-inch skillet, over medium heat, in hot olive oil, cook lamb chunks in two batches until well browned on all sides. Remove lamb pieces as they brown.

Return all meat to skillet and stir in wine, garlic, salt, black pepper, complete seasoning, and rosemary. Heat to boiling. Reduce heat to low, cover, and simmer approximately 2½ hours or until lamb is fork-tender, stirring occasionally.

Add tomatoes and olives during the last 5 minutes of cooking and stir. Serve over a bed of white rice.

6 servings

LAMB CHOPS WITH ORANGE GLAZE

10-ounce jar orange marmalade

2 tablespoons butter

2 tablespoons dry sherry

1 garlic clove, minced

1 teaspoon salt

8 lamb chops, cut 1-inch thick

Preheat broiler according to manufacturer's instructions. In a small saucepan, over low heat, combine first 5 ingredients until marmalade melts, stirring frequently.

Place lamb chops on rack in a broiling pan, and broil 10 to 12 minutes until they reach desired doneness, turning once and brushing occasionally with marmalade mixture.

NOTE: You can also add 2 tablespoons of honey to the marmalade mixture.

8 servings

ROAST DUCKLING A LA NARANJADA
(ROAST DUCK WITH ORANGE SAUCE)

My family and I have always preferred dark meat, so rather than chicken, my mom would roast duck. Duck meat is always richer and darker. She used a rack when roasting duck because it is very fatty. She would always roast 2 ducks because their bone structure is much smaller than a chicken or a turkey. Ducklings have a different proportion of meat to bone. Our favorite duck was with an orange sauce, a bowl of puree of malanga, and, of course, sweet fried plantains.

5-pound duck, thawed

Salt and black pepper to taste

For sauce:

2 oranges, 1 juiced, 1 for garnish

2 teaspoons cornstarch

¼ teaspoon salt

¼ cup sugar

1 chicken-flavor bouillon cube

2 tablespoons brandy

Clean duck, removing giblets and neck, rinse and pat dry. Remove any excess fat from cavity and cut off neck skin. Cut duck into quarters and season with salt and black pepper.

On roasting rack, place pieces skin side down and place pan in a preheated oven at 350°F. Roast for 1 hour, turn pieces, and roast another 45 minutes. If you have a thermometer, place it in the thickest part of the drumstick. Temperature should register between 185 and 190°F.

About 20 to 25 minutes before duck is done, prepare sauce. In a measuring cup, squeeze 1 orange and add water to the juice to make 1 cup. Stir in cornstarch and salt. Stir until completely dissolved and put aside.

In a medium-sized saucepan, over medium heat, heat sugar until melted and golden brown. Stir frequently, and be careful not to burn the sugar. Remove from heat and let stand about 5 minutes.

Add chicken-flavor bouillon cube and orange mixture to sugar and cook another 5 minutes. Make sure sugar is completely dissolved. Stir in brandy and keep sauce warm until ready to serve. Put the duck on a platter and pour sauce over duck. Use the remaining orange to garnish.   *3 to 4 servings*

PORK CHOPS

8 pork chops, ¾-inch thick
⅛ teaspoon salt
⅛ teaspoon black pepper
4 tablespoons olive oil
1 cup onions, finely chopped
4 garlic cloves, minced
16-ounce can tomatoes, diced, reserve
    liquid

8-ounce can mushrooms
1 bay leaf
½ teaspoon dried oregano
½ teaspoon dried basil
1 small green bell pepper, cut into
    thin strips

Season pork chops with salt and black pepper. In a frying pan, heat oil over medium heat. Add pork chops and brown on both sides. Remove and set aside.

In same pan, sauté onions and garlic for about 3 to 5 minutes. Add tomatoes with their liquid, mushrooms, bay leaf, oregano, and basil, and cook for about 5 minutes.

Return chops to pan and top with green pepper strips. Cover, reduce heat to low, and cook until chops are done, approximately 25 minutes.   *8 servings*

MASITAS DE PUERCO FRITAS (FRIED PORK CHUNKS)

Cubans love their pork. It is the official party food, and is used to celebrate Noche Buena [Christmas Eve], and in our family, New Year's Eve was also celebrated with a pork dish. Although rarely, I sometimes make *masitas* as an appetizer for restaurant customers. Our employees have gotten used to it and sometimes make it for their employee meal. They are quick to prepare, crunchy, and delicious.

2-pound pork butt, cut into 2-inch chunks
6 garlic cloves, minced
½ teaspoon salt
½ teaspoon black pepper
1 teaspoon dried oregano
½ cup Seville orange juice or lemon juice
1 cup vegetable oil
Lime juice and salt to taste

Place pork chunks in a mixing bowl, and add garlic, salt, black pepper, oregano, and orange juice. Coat chunks well. Cover bowl and marinate in refrigerator for 1 hour.

In a large skillet, heat oil over medium heat until hot. Discard marinade and add pork chunks to skillet. Cook until golden brown and crispy on all sides. Drain chunks on a paper towel. Sprinkle salt and squeeze lime juice over them.

6 to 8 servings

LECHÓN ASADO (ROAST PORK WITH MOJO SAUCE)

4- to 6-pound Boston butt
4 Seville oranges, juiced
½ cup olive oil
4 tablespoons Badia complete seasoning
4 tablespoons garlic, minced
4 tablespoons dried basil
4 tablespoons dried oregano
4 tablespoons onion powder
2 cups chablis
½ cup water
1 bottle Goya mojo criollo or Badia mojo marinade

Rinse pork butt and put in a large roasting pan.

In a large bowl, mix all other ingredients together with a whisk. Pour half of this mixture over the butt, turn it over, and pour remaining mixture over the other side.

Cook butt fat side down and covered with aluminum foil. Cook at 350°F for 3½ to 4 hours, depending on size. When pork butt is done, the bone should easily pull out.

To make extra mojo sauce, in a medium saucepan put all of the sauce ingredients above, except use only 1 cup of chablis and do not use any water. Bring to a boil.

NOTE: Do not use drippings from the pan for the mojo sauce.   *8 servings*

FRIJOLES COLORADOS CON PUERCO
(RED BEANS WITH PORK)

1 pound dry red beans

6 cups water

1 pound fresh boneless pork

3 garlic cloves, chopped

1½ teaspoons salt

¼ teaspoon black pepper

¼ teaspoon ground oregano

¼ teaspoon cumin

¼ teaspoon ground laurel

1 Seville orange, juiced

½ cup olive oil

1 large onion, diced

1 large green bell pepper, diced

8 ounces tomato sauce

½ cup red pimentos, chopped

¼ cup dry wine

Soak the beans in 6 cups of water for approximately 4 hours.

Cut the pork in 2-inch pieces. Marinate with the chopped garlic, salt, black pepper, oregano, cumin, and laurel. Add the juice from the Seville orange and marinate in refrigerator.

Cook the beans in the same water for about 45 minutes or until beans are halfway tender.

Remove meat from marinade and, in another pot, braise pork, in olive oil, over medium heat until brown. Add the diced onion, green pepper, tomato sauce, chopped pimentos, and dry wine. Cook for another 5 minutes.

Add the pork mixture to the undrained beans. Cover and cook on low heat for approximately 35 to 40 minutes.   *8 servings*

PATAS DE PUERCO CON GARBANZOS
(PIG'S FEET WITH GARBANZO BEANS)

6 pig's feet, cut in half lengthwise

6 cups water

⅓ cup olive oil

1 large onion, finely chopped

2 green bell peppers, finely chopped

3 garlic cloves, finely chopped

¼ pound ham, cubed

1 chorizo, sliced

2 bay leaves

1 teaspoon cumin

½ teaspoon salt

¼ teaspoon black pepper

¼ teaspoon oregano

½ cup tomato sauce

1 can garbanzo beans, drained

½ cup dry wine

½ cup stuffed olives

⅓ cup raisins

Cook pig's feet in 6 cups of water, on high heat, until tender, approximately 1½ to 2 hours. Reserve 3 cups of this water.

In oil, sauté onion, green pepper, garlic, ham, and chorizo. Add bay leaves, cumin, salt, black pepper, oregano, tomato sauce, garbanzo beans, and wine, and cook for approximately 5 to 7 minutes.

Then add the stuffed olives, raisins, reserved water, and the pig's feet. Cover and cook another 10 to 15 minutes at medium heat.   *6 servings*

ARROZ CON CHORIZO (RICE WITH CHORIZO)

My mom often made this dish. It is a nice meal by itself, or you can add a salad.

½ cup olive oil

5 medium chorizos, cut into ¼-inch
    rounds

1 large onion, finely chopped

1 medium green bell pepper, seeded
    and finely chopped

3 garlic cloves, minced

1 teaspoon onion powder

1 bay leaf

1 cup canned diced tomatoes, drained

½ cup sherry

¼ teaspoon bijol or yellow food coloring

2 teaspoons salt

½ teaspoon black pepper

2 cups long grain white rice, washed
    and drained

3 cups water

In a medium-sized saucepan, over low heat, heat the oil for 1 to 2 minutes. Add chorizo, onion, green pepper, and garlic, and stir occasionally for 6 to 7 minutes.

Add onion powder, bay leaf, diced tomatoes, and sherry. Cook about 10 minutes. Increase heat to high, add bijol, salt, black pepper, rice, and water. Bring to a boil.

Reduce heat to low, cover, and simmer until rice is tender, approximately 35 minutes, stirring several times until rice is done. Transfer to a platter and serve.

4 to 6 servings

SUMMER DILL CHICKEN

3 medium whole chicken breasts, cleaned and halved	3 tablespoons brandy
½ cup all-purpose flour	2 teaspoons lemon juice
3 tablespoons salad oil	1½ cups water
3 tablespoons butter	2 chicken-flavor bouillon cubes
2 tablespoons flour	1 cup sour cream
¾ teaspoon salt	1 can artichokes, drained
⅛ teaspoon white pepper	Fresh dill for garnish
½ tablespoon Badia complete seasoning	1 tablespoon dried chives

On waxed paper, coat chicken with ½ cup flour. In a 12-inch skillet, over medium heat, cook chicken in salad oil until lightly browned on all sides. Place chicken in a 12-by-9-inch baking dish and set aside.

Preheat oven to 350°F. In a large saucepan, over low heat, melt butter and stir in 2 tablespoons of flour with salt, white pepper, and complete seasoning until smooth.

Gradually stir in brandy, lemon juice, water, and chicken-flavor bouillon cubes. Cook, stirring occasionally, until thick and smooth. With a wire whisk, blend in sour cream.

Pour mixture over chicken. Cover baking dish with aluminum foil and bake for 45 minutes.

Add artichokes to chicken, cover, and bake another 20 minutes. Garnish with dill and chives.

6 servings

CHICKEN WITH ENDIVE SPEARS

½ cup water

5 tablespoons butter

4 whole chicken breasts, skinned and
    deboned

1 teaspoon salt

4 Belgian endives, trimmed

2 tablespoons lemon juice

2 tablespoons capers, drained

½ cup Italian bread crumbs

1 tablespoon all-purpose flour

2 tablespoons water

1 cup Swiss cheese, shredded

In a skillet, over medium-low heat, heat ½ cup water and 3 tablespoons butter until melted. Arrange chicken in skillet, sprinkle with salt, and place 1 endive on each breast. Sprinkle endive with lemon juice. Cover skillet, and simmer 30 minutes or until endive and chicken are fork-tender.

Leave the liquid in skillet on low heat. Remove endive-topped chicken to a platter. Sprinkle with capers.

Meanwhile, in a small skillet, over medium heat, cook 2 tablespoons butter and bread crumbs until crumbs are lightly browned, stirring frequently. Set aside.

In a cup, blend 1 tablespoon flour and 2 tablespoons water until smooth, and gradually stir into the hot liquid in the skillet. There should be about ⅔ cup liquid left in the skillet.

Cook over medium heat, stirring constantly until mixture is thickened. Remove from heat and stir in Swiss cheese until melted. Pour over chicken, top with bread crumbs, and serve immediately.
4 servings

ARROZ CON POLLO A LA CHORRERA
(CHICKEN AND YELLOW RICE)

This is my favorite. My mom made this every time we had family and friends visit. It is a great party food, and it is very easy to make in large quantities. At Habana Café, I have people calling shortly after 10 A.M. to reserve theirs for that evening because I always run out. No matter how much I make, it never seems to be enough.

A la chorrera means that the rice is very soupy or wet. Most people are not used to eating rice this way, but once they taste it, they are hooked.

3 pounds chicken, skinned and cut into pieces

2 teaspoons salt

½ teaspoon black pepper

1 Seville orange or lemon, juiced

½ cup olive oil

1 large onion, finely chopped

1 large green bell pepper, seeded and finely chopped

4 garlic cloves, minced

1 cup tomato puree

¼ cup pimentos, chopped

1 teaspoon cumin

1 teaspoon oregano

1 bay leaf

1½ cups chablis

4 cups chicken broth

14 ounces Valencia short grain rice

½ teaspoon bijol or yellow food coloring

1 cup drained sweet peas

1 can whole-spear asparagus for garnish

Wash chicken and put into a large bowl. Sprinkle with salt, black pepper, and orange or lemon juice. Set aside to marinate.

In a very large, shallow pan, like a *paellera*, heat ½ cup of olive oil over low heat for about 2 minutes. Add chicken and brown for 6 to 8 minutes on each side. Remove chicken and set aside.

Add onion, green pepper, and garlic, stirring until onion is transparent, about 5 minutes. Add tomato puree, pimentos, cumin, oregano, and bay leaf. Cook for about 5 minutes, stirring frequently.

Add the chicken and coat well with the mixture. Add chablis and cook about 8 to 10 minutes.

Add chicken broth and bring to a boil. Adjust any of the seasonings at this time. Preheat oven to 350°F.

Add the washed and drained rice and bijol to the chicken mixture and bring to a boil over high heat. Cook until almost all the water has been absorbed, about 15 to 20 minutes. Remove from heat and add peas, cover and put in oven until rice is tender, about 30 minutes.

Transfer chicken and rice to a large serving platter and garnish with well-drained asparagus. Serve immediately.   *4 servings*

ARROZ RELLENO (STUFFED RICE)

2 2½-pound whole chickens
½ teaspoon salt
½ cup butter
1 medium onion, finely chopped
½ teaspoon yellow food coloring
1 cup tomato sauce
½ cup dry wine
4 cups chicken broth
3 cups rice
¼ teaspoon ground cumin

1 bay leaf
¼ teaspoon black pepper
¼ teaspoon ground oregano
1 teaspoon salt

For garnish:
Red pimentos
Green and black olives
Small green peas

Remove gizzards from the chickens; these can be used to make chicken broth. Cook whole chickens in a pot or oven with ½ teaspoon of salt. Take chicken meat off the bones and keep warm.

Melt the butter and sauté onion until golden brown. Add food coloring, tomato sauce, dry wine, chicken broth, rice, and the remaining dry spices. Simmer until rice is cooked.

Take half the rice and place in a greased round mold (bundt-cake style). Place the cooked chicken meat on top of the rice and then cover with remaining rice mixture.

Pack mixture tightly and then invert the mold onto a serving platter. Remove the mold and garnish with chopped red pimentos, sliced green and black olives, and green peas.

8 servings

Paella

Paella is named after the special two-handled pan, called *paellera,* in which it is prepared. You do not have to have a *paellera* to make this dish; any large, shallow pan will do. My aunt Alina makes the best paella I have ever had. When she visits, she always makes it for me. She came up in January for my birthday, and on Sunday, we got up, headed over to the restaurant and began making the paella. We were expecting forty friends and family to feast on it. She used eight pounds of rice and forty lobster tails, and everything else that went with it—the chicken, chorizo, shrimp, mussels, clams, and pork. It was an incredible sight.

She looked at me and said, "Wow, I think I overdid it. There's enough food here for at least eighty people."

"Well, there will be doggie bags and lots of leftovers," I agreed. I had to call for two men to come over and carry it to my house. Aunt Alina and I could not lift it ourselves. We got it home, and shortly after, lunch was served.

My guests were amazed at the size, the aroma, and of course, the flavor. Paella is truly the ultimate party food. It is a spectacular sight. When the party was over, the only thing left was a single mussel at the bottom of the pot. I could not believe it. My mom said people were going back for seconds and thirds. What a great compliment! Enjoy.

AUNT ALINA'S PAELLA

1¼ cups vegetable oil

2 medium onions, finely chopped

2 green bell peppers, finely chopped

4 garlic cloves, minced

2 laurel leaves

1 pound boneless chicken breasts, cut into medium pieces

½ pound boneless pork meat, cut into medium pieces

½ pound boneless ham, cut into medium pieces

1 chorizo, cut into small pieces

1 pound shrimp, peeled and deveined

5 lobster tails, cut in half lengthwise

1 pound clams

1 pound mussels

8 ounces tomato sauce

1 4-ounce can chopped pimentos

2 teaspoons salt

¾ teaspoon black pepper

1 teaspoon cumin

½ teaspoon oregano

4 cups dry white wine

1 teaspoon vinegar

2 pounds rice, long grain or Valencia

1 teaspoon yellow food coloring

4 cups chicken broth

For garnish:

½ cup pimentos, chopped

½ cup sweet green peas, canned

¼ cup fresh chopped parsley

⅓ cup green olives

In a large pot, heat oil, add onions, green peppers, garlic, and laurel leaves. Add chicken, pork, ham, and chorizo. Cook at medium heat until tender, approximately 10 to 15 minutes, stirring occasionally.

Add shrimp, lobster tails, clams, and mussels. Add tomato sauce, pimentos, dry condiments, dry white wine, and vinegar. Simmer for approximately 10 to 12 minutes, until shrimp turn pink and mussels and clams begin to open.

Add rice, food coloring, and chicken broth. Simmer until rice is cooked, approximately 25 to 30 minutes. Decorate with garnish and serve immediately.

NOTE: If you use Valencia rice, you may need to add an additional cup of chicken broth. *10 servings*

MACARONES CON POLLO
(MACARONI WITH CHICKEN)

3 tablespoons oil
1 chorizo, chopped
2 pounds boneless chicken
¼ pound ham, chopped
1 onion, minced
1 garlic clove, minced
8 ounces tomato sauce
½ cup dry wine
½ cup chopped pimentos
1 tablespoon vinegar

1 teaspoon salt
⅛ teaspoon black pepper
⅛ teaspoon cumin
⅛ teaspoon laurel powder
⅛ teaspoon oregano
4 cups chicken broth
1 pound macaroni
½ cup grated Parmesan cheese
⅓ cup cracker crumbs

Heat oil in a large skillet, and brown chorizo and chicken. Add ham, onion, garlic, tomato sauce, wine, pimentos, vinegar, salt, black pepper, cumin, laurel, and oregano. Allow to cook for a few minutes and then add 1 cup of chicken broth. Over medium heat, cook until chicken is tender.

In a saucepan, bring the remaining 3 cups of chicken broth to a boil, add macaroni, and cook for 10 to 15 minutes. Combine cooked macaroni with chicken mixture and pour into an 8-inch cake mold or glass casserole dish. Sprinkle the grated Parmesan cheese and cracker crumbs on top. Bake at 350°F until golden brown, approximately 25 minutes. *8 servings*

✍ VEGETALES ✍

VEGETABLES AND ACCOMPANIMENTS

As for me, I love just about any vegetable except for beets. I have had an aversion to beets since the embargo was placed on Cuba in 1962. All we ate during those years was rice, fried eggs on white rice, boiled eggs on white rice, and beets. Yuck! I can still eat eggs and rice, but beets, no way. You will not find a single beet recipe in this book.

Traditional accompaniments to Cuban dishes are black beans and white rice, ripe or green plantains, yuca, and malanga, to name a few. Being Americanized, however, I truly love asparagus, mushrooms, and potatoes. Some of the following recipes are ones I use when I teach cooking classes to benefit the Museum of Fine Arts and when I entertain at home. Some are staples that I only use at the restaurant. The main entrees at Habana Café come with sweet fried plantains, and from time to time, I will also offer yuca with mojo sauce, but it is not as popular. For a while, I added green plantains to the entrées, in addition to the sweet plantains. Some of my carryout customers were calling from home to ask about the "flying saucer" thing they found in their food containers. Needless to say, I stopped including the green plantains. I realize that a lot of these foods are an acquired taste. People hesitate to try them, but once they do, they often love them. One customer who called to inquire about the "flying saucer" called back to say she really liked it and was glad she tried it because it was not something she would have ordered on her own.

FRIED SWEET PLANTAINS

3 medium plantains (skin should be   6 cups vegetable oil
   almost black)

Peel plantains and slice diagonally to ¼-inch thickness.

In a 12-inch skillet, over medium-high heat, heat about 2 inches of oil until very hot. Fry as many slices as will fit in 1 layer. Fry until golden brown on both sides, about 2 to 3 minutes. Drain plantains on a tray covered with paper towels to absorb grease. Transfer to a serving platter and serve immediately.

6 servings

FUFÚ DE PLÁTANOS
(MASHED PLANTAINS)

This is a very ethnic dish, and it can be served alone or as a side dish. I particularly like this with Palomilla Steak. If I am not really hungry, I will eat just a big bowl of this, because it is one of my favorites.

1 green plantain   3 strips of bacon, fried extra crispy
2 semiripe plantains   and chopped
3 tablespoons olive oil   Salt and black pepper to taste

Cut the unpeeled plantains into chunks, 2- to 3-inches thick. Place in a pot filled with enough water to cover plantains. Bring to a boil, reduce heat to medium, and cook for 15 minutes, or until fork-tender.

Drain plantains. When they are cool enough to handle, slash the skin with a knife and peel. Put plantains in a bowl and mash them like potatoes. Add olive oil and bacon and keep mashing until they look like lumpy mashed potatoes. If you find that you need more olive oil, you can add more to moisten. Season with salt and black pepper to taste.

6 to 8 servings

The Habana Café in Gulfport, Florida.

The dining room at Habana Café.

Salmon on Mini-Bagel Crisps, page 12.
Background, Endive with Herbed Goat Cheese, page 9.

Cuban Sandwich, page 10, with a side of Black Beans and Rice, page 81.

Ham Croquettes,
page 16.

Spanish Salad, page 29.

Fillet of Fish Breaded in Plantain Chips, page 34.

Lobster Thermidor, page 37.

Shrimp Ajillo, page 38.

Picadillo, page 40.

Palomilla Steak, page 42.

Boliche (Stuffed Pot Roast), page 44.

Lechon Asado (Roast Pork with Mojo Sauce), page 52.

Arroz con Pollo a la Chorrera (Chicken and Yellow Rice), page 56.

Aunt Alina's Paella, page 59.

Flan de Leche, page 85.

Chocolate Mousse, page 89.

Mojito,
page 101.

Red Sangria, page 105.

Café con Leche, page 107.

Josefa Gonzalez-Hastings serves fillet of fish
breaded in plantain chips, page 34.

PLÁTANOS EN TENTACIÓN
(BAKED SWEET PLANTAINS)

When you taste this side dish, you will think it is in the wrong section of the book. Technically, it is a side dish and not a dessert, but if you want to serve it as a dessert, that is fine too. Pair this with Shrimp Creole and you will love it.

3 ripe plantains
⅓ cup white sugar
⅓ cup brown sugar

3 teaspoons butter
⅛ teaspoon cinnamon
3 teaspoons brandy

Preheat oven to 375°F. Grease a baking pan and place peeled plantains in it. Sprinkle plantains with sugars, and add butter, cinnamon, and brandy.

Bake for approximately 45 minutes, or until golden brown. Check occasionally.
6 servings

YUCA CON MOJO
(YUCA WITH MOJO SAUCE)

2 bags frozen yuca
1½ teaspoons salt
½ cup olive oil
8 garlic cloves, minced

1 medium onion, sliced
*½ cup Seville orange juice or lemon
   juice*

In a large saucepan, over medium heat, cover yuca with water and add ½ teaspoon salt. Bring to a boil. Cover and simmer until very tender. Drain, transfer yuca to a serving platter, and keep warm.

In a medium saucepan, heat olive oil over medium heat until hot, add minced garlic, onions, remaining teaspoon salt, and citrus juice. Stir until onions are cooked. Immediately pour mixture over yuca and serve.

NOTE: If you would like to use fresh yuca, you must peel them and cut into chunks before cooking.
6 servings

MALANGA PUREE

4 medium malanga, peeled and cut into
   1½-inch chunks
4 tablespoons butter

Salt and black pepper to taste
¼ cup evaporated milk
¼ cup whole milk

In a large saucepan, boil malanga until fork-tender, as if you are making mashed potatoes. Drain. Stir in butter, salt, black pepper, evaporated milk, and whole milk. Mash. You can add more milk until you reach a desired consistency. Serve immediately either in a large bowl or in individual servings on plates.

6 servings

ARROZ BLANCO
(WHITE RICE)

White rice—sounds simple enough, right? Well, the first time I attempted to make white rice, it was a disaster. The second time, I thought, I will use minute rice because it cannot possibly go wrong. Well, I burned it. My husband, David, looked at me like I was the bearded lady at the circus.

"How could you burn minute rice?" he asked me. I just shrugged my shoulders, pulled out two potatoes, put them in the microwave, and we had baked potatoes instead.

The next day, I went out and bought an electric rice cooker. Ever since, I have made perfect rice. At the restaurant, I have a gas rice cooker that is commonly used in a lot of Asian restaurants. It makes perfect rice every time. The following recipe is my aunt Alina's, because she makes perfect rice every time, too.

4 cups water
3 tablespoons olive oil
2 teaspoons salt

2 cups long grain white rice, washed
   and drained

In a large, nonstick saucepan, bring water to a boil over high heat. Add olive oil and salt. Add rice and stir. Cook until most of the water has been absorbed, about 10 to 15 minutes.

Stir the rice, cover, reduce heat to low, and cook until rice is fluffy, about 10 to 12 minutes.

4 servings

MOROS Y CRISTIANOS (BLACK BEANS AND RICE)

This literally translates to "Moors and Christians." Legend has it that this dish came to be as a result of the Catholics running the dark-skinned Moors from Spain. The Spanish, who colonized Cuba, are said to have created this dish in honor of those events in Spain. I do not serve this dish at the restaurant, but I would if the Hispanic population here were larger. In the seven years I have been here, only one person, an American, has asked me for it, and he asked for "Morris and Cristo." I have to admit, I was baffled by that name. I had no earthly idea what he was talking about. He looked at me and said, "Well of course you don't know what Morris and Cristo are, you're not Cuban."

"Well, sir, actually I am Cuban," I said.

"Funny, you don't look Cuban," he replied, and I hear that from a lot of people. So, he went on to explain what it was, and I said, "Oh, Moros y Cristianos."

His wife looked at him and said, "It sounds a lot better when she says it."

I joked, "Yeah, I don't know who Morris and Cristo are."

½ pound black beans

7 cups water

2 whole onions, 1 halved, 1 chopped

2 whole green bell peppers, 1 halved,
   1 chopped

4 cups liquid, from the black beans

¾ cup olive oil

¼ pound salted pork, cut in 1-inch pieces

½ pound ham, cut in 1-inch pieces

4 garlic cloves, chopped

¼ teaspoon oregano

¼ teaspoon cumin

1 pound rice

Salt and black pepper to taste

2 laurel leaves

Soak beans in 7 cups of water for approximately 1 hour. Cook beans over medium heat, add halved onion and halved green pepper.

When beans are soft, measure 4 cups of the liquid to make the rice. Discard excess liquid.

In a frying pan, add olive oil, and sauté pork and ham and chopped onions, green peppers, and garlic. Add the oregano and cumin. Mix well as it cooks. Add this mixture to the drained beans.

Add the 4 cups of liquid to the rice, salt, black pepper, and laurel leaves. Bring to a boil and cover. Simmer until rice is tender, approximately 30 to 45 minutes.

6 to 8 servings

MASHED BUTTERNUT SQUASH

2 small butternut squash
2 cups water
1 teaspoon salt

2 tablespoons butter
¼ cup packed brown sugar

Cut squash in half lengthwise and remove all seeds.

In a 10-inch skillet, over medium-high heat, heat 2 cups of water to a boil. Place squash in skillet skin side up and add ½ teaspoon salt. Reduce heat to low, cover, and simmer for 15 minutes until squash is tender. Drain all water and set squash aside to cool.

Scoop pulp out into a large bowl. With a mixer on low speed, mix pulp with ½ teaspoon salt, 2 tablespoons butter, and brown sugar. Mix until smooth. Keep over medium heat until heated through.   *6 servings*

ASPARAGUS WITH WHITE BUTTER SAUCE

24 asparagus stalks, trimmed
6 shallots, peeled and finely minced
¾ cup white wine vinegar

3 sticks unsalted butter, cut into
  1-inch pieces
Salt and white pepper to taste

Prepare asparagus by steaming stalks for about 5 minutes, depending on thickness. Cook until fork-tender.

In a medium saucepan, simmer shallots in vinegar for about 10 minutes. Remove from heat and slightly cool.

Strain and reserve vinegar. Whisk butter, a tablespoon at a time, into the vinegar until smooth. The mixture should be the consistency of a very thin mayonnaise. Season with salt and white pepper to taste. Use immediately or keep warm in a bain-marie, or in any shallow pan large enough to hold the saucepan while filled with 1 inch of hot water.

You should not reheat mixture because butter will separate. Serve asparagus immediately and spoon sauce on top.   *6 servings*

MUSHROOMS WITH SOUR CREAM

½ cup butter
2 pounds sliced mushrooms
½ cup scallions, peeled and diced
1 teaspoon salt

½ teaspoon black pepper
½ teaspoon Badia complete seasoning
½ cup sour cream

In a large skillet, over medium heat, melt butter and add mushrooms, scallions, salt, black pepper, and complete seasoning. Cook, stirring frequently, until mushrooms are tender, about 8 to 10 minutes. Stir in sour cream and heat thoroughly. Do not boil. Spoon mushroom mixture into a bowl and serve.

8 to 10 servings

HOLLANDAISE SAUCE

This is one of my favorite sauces. I commonly use it with Lobster Thermidor and asparagus. Nothing is as good as homemade, but if you are short on time, Knorr has an excellent hollandaise product that comes in an envelope.

3 egg yolks
2 tablespoons lemon juice

½ cup butter
¼ teaspoon salt

You will need a double boiler for this recipe. With a wire whisk, beat egg yolks and lemon juice until well mixed. Place in a double boiler. The bottom should contain hot, but not boiling, water.

Add ⅓ of the butter to the eggs and whisk constantly until butter is melted. Keep adding butter in thirds until gone. Mixture should be thick and heated thoroughly. Remove from heat, add salt, and stir. Keep warm until ready for use.

Yield ⅔ cup

POTATOES AU GRATIN

3 tablespoons butter

6 medium potatoes, peeled and thinly
    sliced

1½ teaspoons salt

1 cup cheddar cheese, shredded

½ cup Vigo bread crumbs

In medium saucepan, melt butter to coat a 12-by-8-inch baking dish. Preheat oven to 425°F. Arrange potatoes in even layers in a baking dish. Sprinkle with salt, cheddar cheese, and bread crumbs. Cover with foil and bake for 20 minutes. Uncover and bake an additional 15 minutes until potatoes are tender.

6 servings

POSTRES

DESSERTS

What's not to love? Desserts are the grand finale to the perfect meal.

Gum was one of my favorite desserts as a child in Cuba. My aunts were already living in the United States, and they would send letters to us with Chiclets inside. My mom would let me chew each piece for 15 minutes a day, then she wrapped it up, and gave it to me again the next day. She would do this until each piece disintegrated. I loved it, because gum was such a novelty to me.

In general, Cubans love their desserts followed by a *cafesito,* and the men have a cigar, a brandy, and a game of dominoes. My mom and I love making desserts even if some of them are time consuming. Desserts look elegant in just about any setting, but I believe it is important to garnish them in some way. I use a lot of edible flowers, orange peels, strawberries, whipped cream, chocolate sauce, and confectioners'(powdered) sugar. This makes the desserts even more appealing to the eye.

FLAN DE LECHE

Flan is a staple at Habana Café, and my mom and family friend Maritza Smith usually make the flan for my restaurant. I came up with a cream cheese variation to our traditional flan recipe, and entered my recipe in the 2003 *Southern Living* Cook-off. To my amazement, I was selected from over 35,000 entries as one of fifteen overall finalists, and one of three finalists in the "Signature Desserts" category. In September of 2003, I headed to Nashville, Tennessee, for the cook-off, which was hosted by NBC's "Today Show" weatherman, Al Roker, and would later air on the Food Network channel.

I had a great time at the three-day event, and the winners were announced at the show taping on the final day of the cook-off. Signature Desserts was the last of the categories to be judged. I was shocked and thrilled to hear Al Roker call my name on stage and announce that my Cream Cheese Flan was the $10,000 grand prize winner of the 2003 Signature Desserts category.

Since then, I have made a lot of cream cheese flans for the media and customers who want to sample the winning recipe. For all flans, you have to get the caramelizing of the sugar just right or you can burn it very easily. With the distractions of a busy restaurant, I have burned the sugar many times. Try both of these recipes, and the results will be well worth the effort.

6 ounces whole milk	*4 egg whites*
1 12-ounce can evaporated milk	*1½ teaspoons vanilla extract*
1 12-ounce can condensed milk	*⅛ teaspoon salt*
7 egg yolks	*1½ cups sugar*

In a large mixing bowl, add all ingredients, except sugar, and mix well with a wire whisk. Drain through a sieve into another bowl and set aside.

Preheat oven to 350°F. Place a pan, large enough to hold a 9-inch ovenproof mold, into the oven and fill about ⅓ of the pan with warm water (a bain-marie). After you have placed the mold in the pan, the water should reach halfway up the mold.

For the caramel:
In a medium-sized, heavy saucepan, over medium heat, cook 1½ cups sugar. After sugar begins to bubble, stir with a whisk constantly until sugar caramelizes to a liquid, golden brown color, approximately 2 to 3 minutes. Be careful not to overcook because sugar burns very quickly.

Pour caramelized sugar into the ovenproof mold and swirl around to coat the bottom and sides of the mold with the sugar. Let mold stand until the sugar hardens.

Pour the flan mixture into the mold, and cover tightly with aluminum foil. Set mold in center of the bain-marie and cook for 1½ hours. Cool to room temperature and then refrigerate for 3 to 4 hours.

To serve:

Run a knife around the inside edges of the mold. Invert the custard onto a serving platter. Scrape out any caramel that may be left for extra caramel sauce.

8 servings

CREAM CHEESE FLAN

Follow the preceding recipe for flan, except instead of adding the 4 egg whites to the mix, add them to 8 ounces of cream cheese and an additional ½ cup sugar.

Blend this in a blender at medium speed until all ingredients are smooth.

Add this to the already prepared mixture. Mix with a wire whisk.

This might require an additional 15 minutes of cooking time. Check the water in the oven and add some hot water if needed.　　*8 servings*

DULCE GRIEGO (POUND CAKE WITH WALNUTS)

1 cup butter, softened
2 cups sugar
4 eggs
1 cup milk
2 cups flour
2 teaspoons baking powder

For the syrup:
2 cups water
2 cups sugar

For garnish:
Confectioners' sugar
Ground cinnamon
Chopped walnuts

Mix softened butter and sugar and beat until creamy. Add eggs one at a time, milk at room temperature, and the flour and baking powder. Beat by hand until well mixed.

Butter a 13-by-9-inch baking mold, pour mixture into it, and bake at 350°F for 1 hour. Test for doneness with a toothpick.

When cool, use a toothpick to make holes throughout the cake.

To make syrup, combine water with sugar and bring to a boil. Simmer for approximately 10 minutes. Add the hot syrup to the cake.

Sprinkle with confectioners' sugar, cinnamon, and walnuts.　　*8 servings*

GUAVA MOUSSE

You can garnish this with pineapple, mint, raspberries, or strawberries. There are many varieties of frozen fruit pulps that you can use to make different flavors of mousse.

1 medium can guava, well drained   *10–12 teaspoons confectioners' sugar*
½ cup heavy cream

Place guava in a blender and puree. Press mixture through a sieve to strain any remaining liquid. Cover and refrigerate.

  With a hand mixer, whip heavy cream until it starts thickening. Add confectioners' sugar and continue to mix until firm peaks form. Fold guava mixture into whipped cream and serve in individual goblets.   *4 servings*

RUM MOUSSE

This is, like all mousses, very light and creamy, and the perfect ending to a meal. This is very easy to make, not at all complicated. If you prefer another flavor, you can substitute virtually anything for the rum: chocolate, Grand Marnier, or Kahlua, for example.

2 cups heavy whipping cream   *3–4 tablespoons rum*
⅓ cup sugar   *Fresh mint or fruit for garnish*

In a large bowl, either glass or stainless steel, add cream and sugar. With a hand mixer on high speed, beat cream and sugar until peaks begin to form. Add rum and mix a few seconds longer until well blended. Spoon mixture into individual goblets and refrigerate for 1 hour before serving. Garnish with fresh mint or fruit, if desired.   *4 servings*

STRAWBERRY RUM MOUSSE

2 packages Knox unflavored gelatin
½ cup water
10 ounces frozen strawberries, thawed
1 cup sugar

2½ cups heavy whipping cream, divided
½ cup light rum
Fresh berries for garnish

Soften gelatin in ½ cup water. Heat over low heat until completely dissolved. Cool to room temperature.

In a blender, add strawberries and sugar and mix well. Add cooled gelatin and mix well. Refrigerate until mixture starts to set.

In a large bowl, whip 1½ cups cream until stiff peaks begin to form. Remove strawberry mixture from refrigerator and add rum. Mix well.

Start folding strawberry mixture into whipped cream until all is used.

Pour into decorative glasses or wine goblets and whip the remaining cream until stiff peaks form. Use this and fresh berries for garnish.   *4 servings*

CHOCOLATE MOUSSE

1 bag chocolate chips
2¼ cups heavy whipping cream

1⅓ cups confectioners' sugar

In a medium saucepan, over low heat, melt chocolate chips in ¼ cup heavy whipping cream, stirring frequently until chocolate is completely melted. It will look like chocolate sauce. Remove from heat and let stand at room temperature.

In a large mixing bowl, add 2 cups heavy whipping cream and mix with a hand mixer on high speed, until it starts getting firm. Add sugar and continue to mix until stiff peaks form. You can adjust the sugar in the whipping process if you would like to use more or less.

Slowly fold chocolate, as much as you like, into cream until well blended. Refrigerate immediately until ready to serve. Spoon into goblets.   *4 servings*

RASPBERRY MOUSSE

1 quart fresh raspberries
1 cup water
¼ cup Chambord raspberry liqueur

1 quart heavy cream
½ cup confectioners' sugar
Mint for garnish

Cook raspberries (save some for garnish) in water and Chambord until very soft. Strain through a sieve and reserve juice.

Whip the heavy cream until it begins to stiffen and add ½ cup raspberry juice and ½ cup sugar. Continue to mix until all ingredients are well blended. Refrigerate until ready to serve. Spoon into chilled goblets, garnish with fresh mint and raspberries, and serve. *6 servings*

CRÈME FRAÎCHE WITH RASPBERRY PRESERVES

2 tablespoons buttermilk or sour cream
2 cups heavy cream

Raspberry preserves
Mint or fresh fruit for garnish

Add either buttermilk or sour cream to the heavy cream. Mix and let stand uncovered at room temperature for 7 to 8 hours. Cover and refrigerate for 24 hours before serving.

Fill wine glasses ¾ full with the mixture. Swirl raspberry preserves on top and garnish with mint or fresh fruit. *2 servings*

STRAWBERRY PARFAIT

1 pint fresh strawberries, hulled
  and sliced
1 pint fresh raspberries
5 tablespoons confectioners' sugar
4 ounces goat cheese, softened

4 ounces cream cheese, softened
2 tablespoons vanilla yogurt
⅛ teaspoon vanilla extract
Fresh mint and berries for garnish

Toss berries with 3 tablespoons confectioners' sugar and set aside for 30 minutes.

In a medium bowl, combine the goat cheese and cream cheese. Add yogurt, vanilla extract, and remaining sugar, and mix well.

Drain berries and add the berry juice to cheese mixture. Mix until smooth. In a wineglass, layer berries with cheese mixture. Garnish with fresh mint and berries.

4 servings

STRAWBERRIES ROMANOFF

¼ cup triple sec, or any orange-flavored liqueur
¼ cup orange juice
2 tablespoons brandy

1 pint fresh strawberries, hulled and halved, saving some for garnish
½ cup heavy cream
1½ tablespoons confectioners' sugar

In a medium bowl, combine triple sec, orange juice, and brandy. Add strawberries and refrigerate for 1 hour. Occasionally baste the strawberries by spooning the liquid over them.

In another medium bowl, with a mixer at high speed, whip the heavy cream until it starts getting firm. Add sugar until cream forms stiff peaks. Spoon strawberries into wine goblets and top with whipped cream. Always garnish!

4 servings

VANILLA ICE CREAM WITH VERY BERRY SAUCE

2 pints fresh raspberries
2½ pints fresh blueberries
1½ pints fresh blackberries
1½ cups sugar
¾ cup water

2 tablespoons Chambord raspberry liqueur
2 pints vanilla ice cream
Mint and berries for garnish

Combine all berries, sugar, and ¾ cup water and bring to a boil. Reduce heat to low and cook for about 10 minutes, stirring occasionally, until sugar is a syrup and berries have released their juices.

Remove from heat and add Chambord. In individual bowls, put a large scoop of ice cream and pour ¾ cup of stewed berries over ice cream. Garnish and serve immediately.

6 servings

CHERRIES JUBILEE

This was one of my mom's favorite American desserts. As a young woman, she spent her summers studying in the United States. Every time she went to a restaurant, she always finished her meal with cherries jubilee.

2 15½-ounce cans pitted cherries with juice	3 tablespoons unsalted butter at room temperature
½ cup sugar	½ cup kirsch or cherry brandy
	1 pint vanilla ice cream

In a pan, over medium heat, combine cherries and sugar. Stir occasionally until sugar is dissolved and liquid is reduced by half, about 4 to 5 minutes.

Add butter and stir until melted. Add brandy and bring mixture to a boil. The brandy might ignite but will burn itself out.

Divide ice cream into serving bowls and spoon mixture over ice cream. Serve immediately.   *4 servings*

FRUIT SALAD WITH RUM DRESSING

This is a great summer treat. You may pick your favorite fruits to use. I usually use kiwi, strawberries, pineapple, bananas, oranges, and cantaloupe.

Bed of lettuce	¼ cup banana yogurt
Fresh fruit	¼ cup pineapple juice
½ cup shredded coconut for garnish	¼ cup light rum
1 cup heavy whipping cream	1 tablespoon coconut cream

On a bed of lettuce, arrange fruits and sprinkle with shredded coconut.

To make dressing, in a medium bowl, whip cream until thick but not stiff. Fold in yogurt, pineapple juice, rum, and coconut cream. Refrigerate until ready for use. Serve salad with dressing.   *Yield 1¾ cups dressing*

FRUIT AU GRATIN

2½ pounds fresh fruit
8 egg yolks
1 cup sugar

1 pint cream
1 tablespoon kirsch or cherry brandy

Using any combination of fresh fruit you prefer, arrange fruit in ovenproof dishes or in a single pan. I like bananas, strawberries, kiwis, raspberries, and blackberries.

Beat egg yolks with sugar. Heat cream in a saucepan, and bring to a boil. Stir in egg and sugar mixture. Bring this mixture to a boil and add kirsch.

Pour mixture over fruit and put under broiler until cream starts to brown, just a few seconds. Be careful because it can burn very quickly. Serve immediately.   *6 servings*

MANGO CHEESECAKE

Mangos are my favorite fruit. Their origin is Indian, but they are now cultivated in temperate climates such as California and Florida. Mangos are in season May through September, although you can find imported mangos year-round. I make everything from mango mousse to mango shakes to this cheesecake recipe from my aunt Alina. If you like mangos and cheesecake, try this.

2 large mangos
½ cup sugar
2 teaspoons lime juice
1 envelope unflavored gelatin

12 ounces cream cheese, softened
¾ cup sour cream
1 teaspoon vanilla
9-inch graham cracker pie shell

Finely chop 1 mango. There should be about 1¼ cups. Combine mango, sugar, and lime juice. Cover and refrigerate for 20 minutes.

Drain the liquid from the mango, about ½ cup, and reserve. Soften gelatin in mango liquid and dissolve in hot water, according to package directions. Combine dissolved gelatin with mango.

Beat cream cheese until light and then stir in sour cream and vanilla. Fold mango into cheese mixture. Pour mixture into pie shell and refrigerate until firm. Slice the remaining mango for garnish.   *6 servings*

MANGO BUTTER

This is a tropical delight. If you have guests for the weekend or friends for brunch, they will love this. This particular spread is best on good, old-fashioned bread or English muffins. If you want to try it on Cuban bread, make sure the bread is toasted. During the summer months, when mangos are plentiful, I make it myself. Otherwise, Williams-Sonoma sells a great mango butter by American Spoon.

¼ cup softened butter at room temperature

½ cup honey
¼ cup mango, finely chopped

In a medium-sized bowl, mix all 3 ingredients with a spoon or electric mixer. When ingredients are well mixed, transfer to a serving bowl. This will last about a week in the refrigerator.   *Yield 1 cup*

PEACH MELBA

⅔ cup raspberry preserves
2 tablespoons hot water
6 scoops vanilla ice cream

14-ounce can sliced peaches, drained
Fresh mint for garnish

In a small saucepan, dissolve raspberry preserves with 2 tablespoons hot water.
    Put scoops of ice cream in individual goblets and neatly place peach slices on top of ice cream. Drizzle with raspberry mixture, garnish with mint, and serve.

6 servings

RUM BALLS

¼ cup dark rum
1½ cups vanilla wafers, crumbled
¼ cup honey

2 cups ground walnuts
Confectioners' sugar

In a medium bowl, combine all ingredients except sugar.
    Shape mixture into 1-inch balls and roll in confectioners' sugar. Store in a tightly covered container.   *Yield 2½ dozen*

MANZANAS RELLENAS EN ALMENDRAS
(STUFFED APPLES WITH ALMONDS)

6–8 apples

1 cup toasted almonds, chopped

½ cup sugar

2 teaspoons almond extract

½ cup melted butter

2 teaspoons water

3 teaspoons dry wine

Cinnamon powder

Whipped topping or vanilla ice cream
   (optional)

Core apples to make an opening of approximately 1 inch.

In a bowl, mix the almonds, sugar, almond extract, and melted butter. Stuff apples with mixture, using all of it.

Place stuffed apples in a baking dish and add water to the bottom of the dish, not over apples. Pour the dry wine over the stuffed apples.

Bake at 350°F for approximately 1 hour. Sprinkle lightly with cinnamon powder when cool. Serve with whipped topping or vanilla ice cream.

6 to 8 servings

NATILLA
(VANILLA PUDDING)

4 cups milk

1 cinnamon stick

1 piece of lime peel

¼ teaspoon salt

8 egg yolks

1½ cups sugar

4 teaspoons cornstarch

¼ cup water

1 teaspoon vanilla

Cinnamon powder

In a saucepan, mix milk, cinnamon stick, lime peel, and salt. Bring to a boil. Let mixture cool at room temperature.

Beat egg yolks with sugar. Dissolve cornstarch in water and add to egg-yolk mixture.

Add egg-yolk mixture to milk mixture. Put through a sieve and cook, constantly stirring, over medium heat, until mixture has thickened. Add vanilla.

Refrigerate. Before serving, sprinkle with cinnamon powder.   *6 servings*

ARROZ CON LECHE
(RICE PUDDING)

6 cups milk

1 cup rice, medium grained

½ cup sugar

1 piece of lime peel

1 cinnamon stick

1 pinch salt

2 teaspoons vanilla extract

Ground cinnamon for garnish

In a saucepan, add milk, rice, sugar, lime peel, cinnamon stick, and salt. Cook over medium heat until mixture starts bubbling around the edges, stirring frequently. Reduce heat to low, cover and simmer for one hour or until rice is very tender, stirring occasionally.

Stir in vanilla, cover and refrigerate for 4 hours. Before serving, remove lime peel and cinnamon stick. Spoon into dessert dishes and sprinkle with cinnamon.

8 servings

BREAD PUDDING

1 loaf French bread, cut into pieces

12-ounce can evaporated milk

14-ounce can condensed milk

1½ cups half-and-half

1 cup currants or raisins

½ cup dark rum

4 tablespoons butter, melted

½ teaspoon vanilla

2 teaspoons cinnamon

In a large bowl, add all ingredients and let soak until bread has absorbed all liquid, approximately 15 to 20 minutes. If it seems dry, add an additional ¼ to ½ cup half-and-half. Place in a 12-by-9-inch mold.

Preheat oven to 350°F. Cook about 1 hour. Check for doneness by inserting a knife into the center of the pudding. Pudding is done when knife comes out clean. Serve warm or cold, and topped with Light Rum Sauce (recipe follows).

10 servings

LIGHT RUM SAUCE

1½ cups sugar
1 cup water
2 tablespoons butter

½ teaspoon cinnamon
¼ cup Jamaican rum

Bring sugar and water to a boil, making sure sugar is dissolved. Add butter and cinnamon, and cook until butter is melted. Add rum and stir, cooking for 1 minute. Serve warm over Bread Pudding.   *Yield 1½ cups*

BEBIDAS

BEVERAGES

Cuba—The Island of Rum

Rum was not always the choice liquor in Cuba, as it only appeared about 150 years ago, and the Spanish settlers preferred wine.

One of the first crops planted by the Spanish was sugarcane to produce sugar and molasses to use as sweeteners. As the sugar industry grew in Cuba, so did the residues from the manufacturing process. The slaves and the poor began using this residue to make liquor. The alcohol they produced was so potent that they watered it down, and it was still potent. They called it *aguardiente* [burning water]. The African slaves used it in their religious rituals, and to this day, it is still being used in the practice of Santería.

The breakthrough for Cuban rum came when an immigrant from Spain, Don Facundo Bacardi, settled in Santiago. He purchased a shop that contained a small still for making rum. After months of hard work and trial and error, he won the prize offered by the government to the person who produced the smoothest and lightest rum.

On February 1862 the Bacardi Company was founded. Soon Cuban rum became the toast of the world, a perfect match to the other famous Cuban product, the cigar. The production of rum was a booming business until October 1960, when Fidel Castro's government nationalized distilleries. The Bacardi family fled in exile to the Bahamas, where they began rebuilding their business.

Throughout the 1960s, the Cuban government continued using the Bacardi label, but when they tried selling the rum abroad, all the bottles were seized because the Bacardi name was trademarked by the family. A lawsuit was filed in the World Court, and the Cuban government lost. They were forced to stop using the Bacardi name.

The Cuban government now produces a rum called Havana Club that is the top of the line. I have a bottle that was given to me as a gift from a customer who visited Cuba. I have never opened it, so I cannot compare it to Bacardi. Customers who visit Cuba tell me that there are about a dozen different brands of rum being produced on the island. Home distilling is quite popular because most people do not have the money to buy rum. One of my employees, Orestes, and his wife, Niurka, who left Cuba five years ago, educate me on the names of these home concoctions. The names lead me to believe that sampling them is flirting with blindness. They are called Chispa de Tren [train sparks], Esperame en el Cielo Corazon [Wait for me in heaven, my love], and Echate para Atras [lean back]. All in all, it is good to hear that the Cuban people of today have not lost their sense of humor and remain very colorful people.

I do not know many Cubans who would turn down the classic mojito or a daiquiri, rum drinks made with crushed ice. Both are perfect for hot Florida nights. When I was a child, my mom often made daiquiris. She always crushed the ice by hand, using a special kitchen towel reserved for this purpose. She would empty a tray of ice cubes onto this towel, fold it over, and use a mallet to crush the ice. My dad would ask her, "Why don't you do that in the blender?" and her reply was always, "It's just not the same."

We had a beautiful pink-tile countertop at the time, but my dad replaced it with Formica because he did not think the tile could stand up to her culinary habits.

The Home Bar

A well-stocked home bar is essential for entertaining. Here is a list of the contents of my home bar:

1 liter bourbon	*2 liters white rum*	*1 fifth Grand Marnier*
1 liter gin	*1 liter dark rum*	*1 fifth Kahlua*
2 liters vodka	*1 fifth dry vermouth*	*2 six-packs light beer*
1 liter whiskey	*1 fifth sweet vermouth*	*1 six-pack dark beer*
2 liters scotch	*1 fifth tequila*	*1 six-pack imported beer*

Mixers: club soda, tonic water, cola, Bloody Mary mix, ginger ale, orange juice
Wines: chardonnay (dry), chablis (dry, fruity), chenin blanc (dry, semisweet), pinot blanc (dry, tart), burgundy (dry, medium bodied), cabernet sauvignon (dry), pinot noir (dry), zinfandel (fruity)

CUBA LIBRE (FREE CUBA)

This was always a favorite in our family. My uncles loved this drink. I remember our visits to my tio Carlos and tia Chirin's house. On weekend nights, the domino games would be going on, and they would break out the cigars and toast with Cuba Libres.

Ice
1½ ounces Bacardi light rum

3 ounces Coca-Cola
2 lime wedges

Fill a glass with ice. Add rum, coke, and the juice of 1 lime wedge. Stir together and garnish with the remaining lime wedge. Serve.   *1 serving*

EL PRESIDENTE

Ice
Fresh mint leaves

1½ ounces Bacardi rum
Canada Dry ginger ale

Fill a tall glass with ice and mint leaves. Add rum and fill the rest of the glass with ginger ale.   *1 serving*

HABANA PINK RUM COCKTAIL

I love the nectars we have at the restaurant. They are readily available in most grocery stores in the ethnic sections. Goya and Sunchy produce some of the best. I was hosting a lunch at my house, and I decided to combine guava, cranberry juice, rum, and triple sec. Everybody enjoyed it.

½ cup guava nectar
¼ cup cranberry juice
1½ ounces rum

½ ounce triple sec
Ice
Colored sugar (optional)

In a cocktail shaker, combine all ingredients except sugar. Stir, then pour into glasses with ice. You can wet the rim of the glasses and then dip them in colored sugar before you pour the drinks.   *2 servings*

HABANA TROPICAL PUNCH

1 bottle Bacardi gold rum	¾ liter grapefruit juice
½ bottle apricot liquor	½ lemon, juiced
¾ liter unsweetened pineapple juice	Fresh fruit for garnish

Combine all ingredients except fruit and refrigerate for 2 hours. Put in a punch bowl, garnish with fresh fruit, and serve over ice. For a beautiful garnish, you can add fruit pieces to individual ice cube trays, fill halfway with water, and freeze. When frozen, fill to the top with water and return to freezer.

10 servings/20 glasses

BLACKBERRY DELIGHT

1½ ounces Bacardi black rum	½ ounce lime juice
1 ounce blackberry brandy	2 cups ice
1 ounce banana liqueur	Fresh blackberries for garnish
½ ounce grenadine	

In a blender, mix all ingredients except the blackberries. Pour into a margarita glass and garnish with fresh blackberries. *1 serving*

The Mojito

The bygone era of elegance in Cuba is over, but it left behind the mojito. Started in 1942 as a grocery store, La Bodequita del Medio became a restaurant after World War II. It was a favorite meeting place for intellectuals, journalists, and writers, such as Hemingway. It became so popular that the owner opened a special area in the back to serve typical Cuban dishes. I have been told that all the walls of La Bodequita are covered with the signatures of patrons. Hemingway signed his, "My mojito in La Bodequita. My daiquiri in El Floridita."

All over the world, people have tried to capture the enchantment of La Bodequita. You can find a La Bodequita in places such as Mexico, California, Paris, and Berlin.

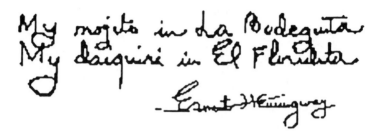

My mojito in La Bodequita
My daiquiri in El Floridita

—Ernest Hemingway

Ernest Hemingway's note and signature on the wall of the La Bodequita.

MOJITO

¼ cup freshly squeezed lime juice
2 ounces Bacardi white rum
2 teaspoons sugar

½ cup crushed ice
4 ounces club soda
Fresh mint leaves

Put all ingredients, except for mint leaves, in a cocktail shaker and stir. Pour into a glass and garnish with fresh mint. If you like it extra minty, stir 1 mint leaf into the shaker.

1 serving

The Daiquiri's Story

The birth of this great classic is unclear. There are two versions as to how the daiquiri was born, and the truth probably lies somewhere in between the two. The first story tells of an engineer who, at the beginning of the twentieth century, visited an iron mine called Daiquiri, located in the east of Cuba. He spoke with an American engineer, and at the end of the day, he suggested to the American that they have a drink. The legend says that when the American opened his storeroom, there was only rum, limes, and sugar. They mixed these ingredients with ice. The American explained that this drink had no name and said, "We'll call it the daiquiri."

The second version says that in 1898, American troops landed in the region called Daiquiri Beach, near Santiago de Cuba. They were intervening in the war between Cuba, the United States, and Spain, and were commanded by General

Shafter. Shafter, by all accounts, was quite the gourmet. In no time, he discovered the drink preferred by the Cuban patriots: rum, lime, and sugar. Shafter added the ice. So, this legend has the daiquiri named by a U.S. soldier in honor of Daiquiri Beach.

El Floridita

The mere mention of that name and my mom's heart melts, her eyes sparkle, and she lets out a schoolgirl sigh. It is like putting her in a time machine that revives her old glory.

"*Recordar es volver a vivir* [To remember is to live again]," she says.

La Piña de Plata [The Silver Pineapple] was established in Habana, Cuba, in 1820. Over time, the number of American tourists was so great, that they persuaded the owner to change the name. In 1898 the name was changed to La Florida, and with time, it became El Floridita. It still exists on the corner of Obispo Street and Monserrate Street. Customers at Habana Café tell me of their visits there. At one end of the bar, where so many stars have visited, a chain protects the bar stool of Ernest Hemingway, unoccupied to this day. On the wall there is his bronze bust, inaugurated in 1954 for the Nobel Prize he won. Visiting this famous bar is like having ringside seats to the heart of what was once the most fascinating city. El Floridita is the cradle of the daiquiri. It is the very ambiance that inspired Hemingway, and he, in a way, immortalized the daiquiri, perhaps the most famous drink in the world.

DAIQUIRI

2 ounces Bacardi white rum	*½ cup crushed ice*
1 ounce freshly squeezed lime juice	*Fresh mint for garnish*
1 teaspoon sugar	

Put all the ingredients except mint into a blender and blend at high speed, until the drink thickens. Pour into a glass, garnish, and serve.   *1 serving*

PINEAPPLE DAIQUIRI

2 ounces Bacardi light rum
1 tablespoon triple sec
½ cup canned, crushed pineapple
1 tablespoon lime juice

1 tablespoon sugar
½ cup crushed ice
Fresh mint and pineapple slices for
  garnish

In a blender, combine all ingredients except mint and pineapple slices and blend at high speed until smooth. Taste and add more ice or sugar if needed. Pour into a glass and serve immediately. Garnish with fresh mint and slices of pineapple.

1 serving

BANANA DAIQUIRI

1½ ounces Bacardi light rum
1 teaspoon lemon juice
3 teaspoons sugar, or to taste

1 ripe banana
Ice
Mint leaves and cherries for garnish

Put all ingredients except ice, mint, and cherries into a blender and blend for 20 to 30 seconds. Add ice and continue to blend until the mixture is frozen. Garnish with cherries and mint and serve immediately.

1 serving

PEACH DAIQUIRI

½ peach, fresh or canned
3 teaspoons sugar
½ ounce lemon juice

1½ ounces Bacardi light rum
½ cup ice
Peach slices and mint leaves for garnish

In a blender, add all ingredients except peach slices and mint and blend well until it has the consistency of a frappé. Garnish with peach slices and fresh mint and serve immediately.

1 serving

SANGRIA

½ cup sugar
¼ cup lemon juice
½ cup orange juice
¼ cup brandy

3½ cups burgundy wine
7 ounces club soda
Ice
Fruit for garnish

Pour sugar, lemon juice, orange juice, and brandy into a large pitcher. Stir until sugar is dissolved. Stir in wine and club soda. Add ice. Garnish with strawberries, grapes, or oranges.

NOTE: For White Sangria, substitute chablis for the burgundy wine and sprinkle with cinnamon. *8 servings*

RUM SANGRIA PUNCH

1 bottle Bacardi light rum
1 liter red wine (burgundy)
1 liter lemonade
1 orange, sliced

4 peaches, sliced
15 strawberries, sliced
1 lime, sliced

Combine liquids with all the fresh fruits, and refrigerate for about 2 hours. Transfer to a punch bowl when ready to serve. If you would like it sweeter, add sugar to taste. *10 servings/20 glasses*

MALTA SHAKE

Another traditional Cuban favorite. Malta is a beverage made of barley malt, corn sugar, molasses, corn, and hops. My favorite malta is Hautey.

¼ cup condensed milk
1 bottle of malta

Ice

In an 8-ounce glass, pour the condensed milk and a little of the malta and stir until milk is dissolved. Fill the rest of the glass with malta, add ice, and enjoy.

1 serving

MANGO SHAKE

Tropical fruit shakes are a favorite with Cuban people. I always keep frozen pulp to make my *batidos* [milkshakes]. Among my favorite pulps are mamey, papaya, and guanábana.

⅔ cup frozen mango pulp

1 cup whole milk

½ cup evaporated milk

2 tablespoons sugar, or to taste

Mango slices for garnish

Combine all ingredients except mango slices in a blender and mix until smooth. Serve in a tall glass and garnish with a fresh slice of mango.

NOTE: To make other fruit shakes, use the same amount of pulp or substitute 1 cup if you like it fruitier.

2 servings

CREMA DE VIE (CREAM OF LIFE)

This is the Cuban version of eggnog. It is rich and creamy, and although my aunts make it with both cognac and rum, I prefer it with just rum.

1 cup water

2 cups sugar

6 egg yolks

1 can condensed milk

½ bottle of Spanish cider, Cidra

½ cup rum or cognac

1 teaspoon of vanilla extract

In a medium pot, stir water and sugar until well mixed. Cook over medium heat for 5 minutes. Remove from heat. Let mixture sit until liquid is room temperature.

In a large mixing bowl, beat the egg yolks and gradually add the condensed milk until well mixed.

Gradually add the sugar mixture, constantly stirring.

Add the cider, rum, and vanilla, stirring constantly. When all is well mixed, drain through a sieve and place in a quart glass container. Refrigerate for at least 3 hours.

Serve cold in a demitasse cup.

10 servings

CAFÉ CON LECHE (COFFEE WITH MILK)

Cubans love their coffee, and no matter how great the meal, if you forget the *cafesito* at the end, you have ruined it. My Uncle Julio told me he could not digest his food if he did not have his coffee after a meal. The *cafesito* always has to have *espumita* on top, a creamy golden froth.

My favorite coffee machine is the mini-espresso machine made by Krups. I not only use it at home every morning for my café con leche, but I also use it at the restaurant. They are very durable and are still going after several years of restaurant use. The espresso coffee I use is by Bustello, but this is just my preference. I buy it by the case and refrigerate what I do not use.

1 cup heavy cream
2 tablespoons confectioners' sugar
2 tablespoons cocoa powder
Espresso

¼ cup evaporated milk
½ cup whole milk
Liquer (optional)

Whip cream until it begins to thicken. Add sugar and cocoa powder and continue to whip until stiff peaks form. Cover and refrigerate until ready for use.

Prepare espresso according to manufacturer's directions for your particular machine. Combine evaporated and whole milks, heat, and add to espresso. Top with chocolate mixture. You may also flavor the topping by adding 1 tablespoon of your favorite liqueur, such as Bailey's Irish Cream or amaretto.

1 serving

ICED CAFÉ CON LECHE

Espresso
¼ cup evaporated milk
Whole milk

Ice
Sugar, chocolate syrup, whipped cream,
*   cocoa, and cinnamon to taste*

Prepare espresso.

In a tall tumbler, add ¼ cup evaporated milk. Fill glass with whole milk, leaving room to add ice and espresso. Add sugar and chocolate syrup to taste. Top with whipped cream, and sprinkle with cocoa and cinnamon.   *1 serving*

GLOSSARY

avocado: Known in Spanish as *aguacate*, this fruit is native to the tropics and subtropics and is widely used throughout Latin America. Its flesh is green, and it has a buttery texture. The two most popular types of avocados are the Hass, which has almost black skin, and the Green Fuerte, which has a very thin, smooth green skin.

Badia complete seasoning *[sazon completa]:* This is a product made by a company called Badia, which manufactures common products for Latin cooks. It is readily available in most grocery stores in the spice aisle. A few of the ingredients that give *sazon completa* its flavor are granulated garlic, granulated onion, oregano, parsley, ground cumin, cilantro and monosodium glutamate. You could probably mix these dry ingredients together and come close to this flavor.

basil: This herb is a member of the mint family. Fresh basil has a pungent flavor. It is a key herb in Mediterranean cooking. There are several varieties of basil: opal basil, lemon basil, clove basil, and cinnamon basil. Their fragrance and flavor match their respective names.

bay leaf: It is also called laurel leaf or bay laurel. This herb comes from the evergreen bay laurel tree. There are two main varieties of bay leaf, California and Turkish.

béchamel (BEH-shah-mehl): This is a very basic, French white sauce made by stirring milk into a butter and flour mixture. The thickness depends on the proportion of flour and butter to milk.

bijol (bee HOHL): Bijol is a condiment used to give rice a yellow color. It is made of corn flour, cumin, and annatto. Annatto is a derivative of achiote seed, which has a slightly musky flavor. Achiote seed, in its paste and powder forms, is used in the United States to color butter, margarine, cheese, and smoked fish. It is a substitute for saffron as a food color.

bitter orange: Called *naranja agría* in Spanish, bitter oranges are also known as Seville oranges, and are very popular in the tropics and Mediterranean. This orange tastes very tart and bitter, but it is wonderful for marinating pork and chicken and for making mojo sauce. Bitter oranges are in season all year.

blackened seasoning: This is a Cajun spice mixture that you can rub on food. When the food is cooked in a hot skillet, the seasoned rub gives it an extra crispy crust.

capers: Capers are the flower buds of a bush common to the Mediterranean coast. *Alcaparras* in Spanish, they range in size from very tiny to the size of a cocktail olive. They are very salty and should be rinsed before using. Capers are great in sauces and can be used to garnish certain dishes.

chorizo (chor-EE-zoh): This is a highly seasoned pork sausage. It is used in both Mexican and Spanish cuisines. Mexican chorizo is made with fresh pork, while Spanish chorizo uses smoked pork. The casing should always be removed.

cumin (KUH-mihn, KYOO-mihn): *Comino,* in Spanish, is in the parsley family. With a strong aroma and an earthy flavor, cumin is used in the preparation of many foods. When it is dried, it looks like a caraway seed.

guava (GWAH-vah): Guavas, *guayabas* in Spanish, are tropical fruits that grow in California, Florida, Hawaii, and South America. There are several varieties. If you are going to eat them, they should be very ripe. They also make great jams and preserves. Canned guavas are available in many supermarkets, usually in the ethnic food aisle.

lime: This citrus fruit, along with the Seville orange, is a key ingredient for marinating and flavoring a lot of Cuban dishes.

malanga (ma-LANG-ah): This is a root with white flesh and a rough, brown skin. In the Cuban home, it is used like a potato, mashed or added to soups. Malanga is never eaten raw, and should be peeled and cooked. It has a mild, nutty flavor.

mango: The thin skin of the mango is green. As it ripens, it turns yellow and red. Mango is very exotic tasting. Mangos are in season from May to September. You can peel and eat a plain mango, or use them for chutney or mousse.

mojo (mo-ho): Mojo is a sauce made of garlic, olive oil, onions, and bitter oranges. Mojo is used as a dressing for certain vegetables, like yuca, and as a marinade for chicken, fish, and pork. You can buy mojo in markets, but it is a poor substitute for homemade mojo sauce.

oregano: Also called marjoram, oregano belongs to the mint family. It is a very strong herb and should be used with caution. Mediterranean oregano is milder than the Mexican variety. You can find it dried in many markets, as well as fresh in the produce section. It is also very easy to grow and does not require a lot of maintenance.

paprika: This is a powder made by grinding sweet red pepper pods. You can use it to flavor or garnish.

plantain (PLAN-tain): Plantains, *plátanos* in Spanish, are very large bananas used for cooking. They are used much like the potato is in American cuisine, as a side dish, fried, mashed (called *fufú*), or added to soups. When plantains are ripe, their skin is nearly black. Yellow plantains are semiripe and green plantains are unripened.

saffron: *Azafrán* in Spanish, saffron is the world's most expensive spice because it is very labor intensive to process. Saffron comes from the yellow-orange stigmas of the small purple crocus. Each flower provides three stigmas, which are carefully handpicked and then dried. It takes over fourteen thousand of these tiny stigmas to make an ounce of saffron. It is used to flavor and tint food. It can be purchased in powder form or in threads. The powdered form is much weaker in flavor. Threads should be crushed before using. Saffron should be stored in an airtight container in a cool, dark place. It will keep for up to six months.

sofrito (soh-FREE-toh): Sofrito is made by processing red peppers, green peppers, onions, and garlic in a food processor and then sautéing them in hot olive oil. Sofrito is used to flavor soups and sauces.

yuca (YUHK-uh): Also known as cassava, this is a root vegetable with a tough brown skin and white flesh. Yuca are in season all year. They are used in soups or as a side dish, and should be peeled before using. I recommend the frozen yuca, which is already peeled and ready to boil. Goya has an excellent yuca product.

∽ INDEX ∽

Page references in italic type indicate photographs.

Josefa Gonzalez-Hastings, Jo to her friends, was born in Habana, Cuba, in 1959 to Emilio and Flor Gonzalez. They lived in Cuba until 1965 when they left for Mexico City to await their visas to the United States. In 1966, after nine months in Mexico, they arrived in Miami. They relocated to St. Petersburg that same year and have lived there ever since.

Jo graduated from St. Petersburg College and realized she wanted to travel, so she began a career as an international flight attendant for Eastern Airlines based out of New York and Miami. In 1989, when the labor union called a strike, not knowing what the outcome might be, she applied with American Airlines and was hired. She was based in Dallas, Texas, and lived there for nine months before transferring to Miami as a domestic flight attendant. She married David Hastings in 1991, and they opened the Habana Café in 1997.

Jo credits her culinary talents to instinct and years of learning from her family. *Tampa Bay Magazine* named Jo one of Tampa Bay's top chefs in 2003, and has also awarded Habana Café the Best Cuban Food award every year since 1998. She has also won *Beach Life*'s Best Cuban Food award every year since 1997.

In 2003, Jo was selected as one of fifteen finalists from more than 35,000 entries in the 2003 *Southern Living* Cook-off. The cook-off was hosted by Al Roker of NBC's "Today Show," and held in Nashville, Tennessee. Jo's Cream Cheese Flan recipe won the $10,000 prize in the Signature Desserts category and the $1,000 sponsor award from Philadelphia Cream Cheese. The 2003 *Southern Living* Cook-off was broadcast on the Food Network channel in January 2004, and Jo was also featured in the January issue of *Southern Living* magazine.

Jo spends her free time volunteering for local fund-raisers such as the Florida Orchestra, Museum of Fine Arts, Infinity Club for Abused Children and Adults, the Science Center, the Boley Centers for Behavioral Health, and her favorite charity, Save Our Strays. She has a total of twenty cats and a giant bunny. Her favorite hobbies are cooking and entertaining.

Titles of related interest from University Press of Florida

The Columbia Restaurant Spanish Cookbook
Adela Hernandez Gonzmart and Ferdie Pacheco

The Christmas Eve Cookbook
Ferdie Pacheco and Luisita Sevilla Pacheco

St. Petersburg and the Florida Dream
Raymond Arsenault

The Architecture of Leisure: The Florida Resort Hotels of
Henry Flagler and Henry Plant
Susan R. Braden

Embracing America: A Cuban Exile Comes of Age
Margaret L. Paris

Looking at Cuba: Essays on Culture and Civil Society
Rafael Hernández

For more information on these and other books, visit our
Web site at www.upf.com.